ONE-MINUTE PUZZLES

ONE-MINUTE PUZZLES

Can you solve the puzzles and beat the clock?

ARCTURUS

ARCTURUS

This edition published in 2023 by Arcturus Publishing Limited
26/27 Bickels Yard, 151–153 Bermondsey Street,
London SE1 3HA

Copyright © Arcturus Holdings Limited
Puzzles by Puzzle Press

All rights reserved. No part of this publication may be reproduced, stored in a retrieval system, or transmitted, in any form or by any means, electronic, mechanical, photocopying, recording or otherwise, without prior written permission in accordance with the provisions of the Copyright Act 1956 (as amended). Any person or persons who do any unauthorised act in relation to this publication may be liable to criminal prosecution and civil claims for damages.

ISBN: 978-1-3988-2753-0
AD011093NT

Printed in China

CONTENTS

Introduction 6

One-minute Puzzles 7

Two-minute Puzzles 139

Three-minute Puzzles 173

Solutions 207

Introduction

Challenge your brain with these excellent timed puzzles. Have your stopwatch or smartphone at the ready and see if you can beat the clock. Don't worry if you don't manage them in the allotted time. You may have a particular skill for some puzzles and complete them more speedily, while others take a little longer. You will probably find the ones that seem difficult becoming easier once you have tackled several of them. Just keep trying and see if you can improve your own time or pit your wits against a friend or family member and see who can solve them first!

There are more than 100 one-minute puzzles inside, plus an additional 30 each of two- and three-minute puzzles to give you a tougher challenge once you have mastered the one-minute ones. Keep your wits sharp and give your brain a mental workout as you see if you can solve them all! If you do get stuck, all the solutions are at the back of the book.

1

One to Nine

Using the numbers below, complete these six equations (three reading across and three reading down). Every number is used once.

Make the calculations in the order in which they appear: working from left to right, or top to bottom.

1 2 3
4 5 6
7 8 9

	x		+		=	8
+		x		+		
	−		x	8	=	24
x		−		x		
	+		x		=	42
=		=		=		
28		2		77		

2

Number Crunch

Starting at the top left with the number provided, work down from one box to another, applying the mathematical instructions to your running total.

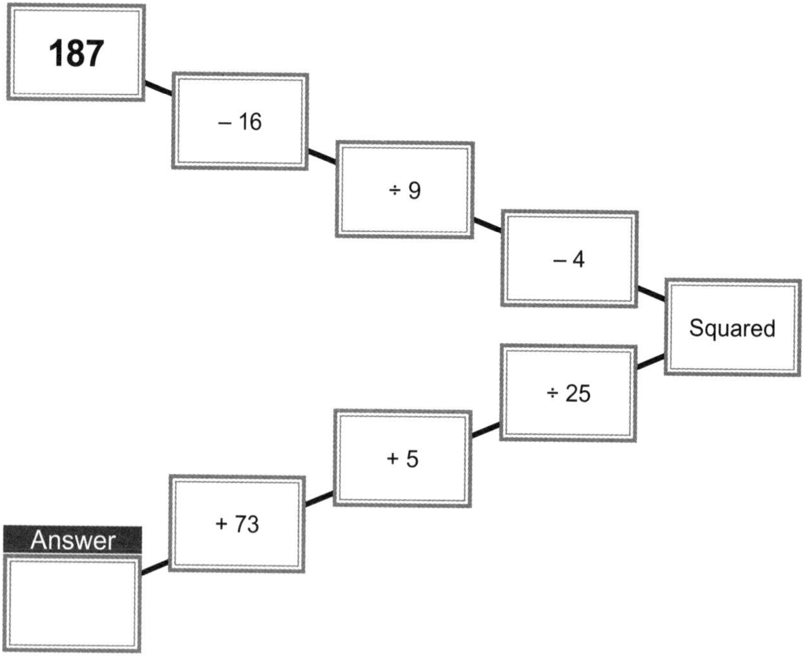

- **187**
- − 16
- ÷ 9
- − 4
- Squared
- ÷ 25
- + 5
- + 73
- Answer

Summing Up

Arrange one of each of the four given numbers, as well as one each of the symbols − (minus), x (times), and + (plus) in every row and column to arrive at the answer at the end of that row or column.

Make the calculations in the order in which they appear: working from left to right, or top to bottom.

4 7 8 9

7	+	9	−	4	x	8	=	96
							=	43
+		x						
							=	34
9							=	20
=		=		=		=		
51		47		48		40		

4

Isolate

Draw walls to partition the grid into areas (some walls are already drawn in for you). Each area must contain two circles, area sizes must match those shown by the numbers above the grid and each "+" must be linked to at least two walls.

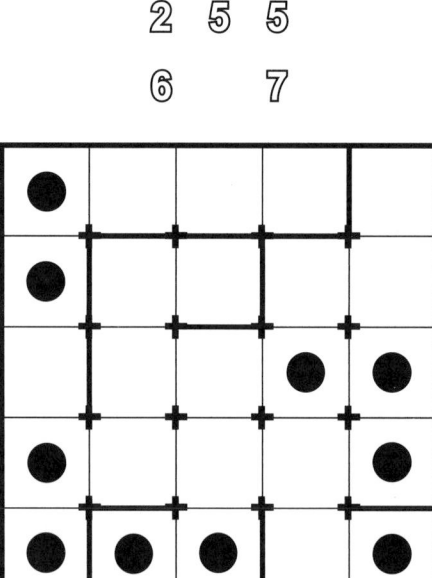

5

Round Up

The number in each circle is the sum of the two numbers below it. Just work out the missing numbers in every circle!

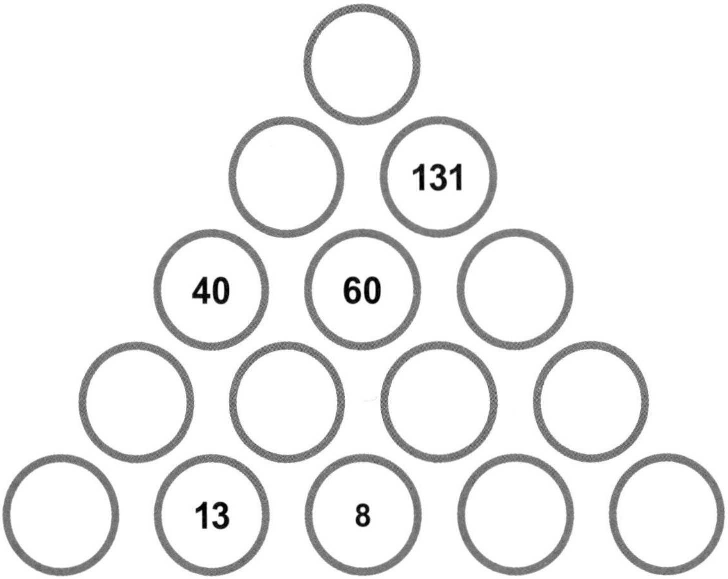

6

One to Nine

Using the numbers below, complete these six equations (three reading across and three reading down). Every number is used once.

Make the calculations in the order in which they appear: working from left to right, or top to bottom.

1 2 3
4 5 6
7 8 9

	+		x		=	50
+		+		+		
	x	4	+		=	13
x		x		x		
	+		−		=	12
=		=		=		
24		88		28		

7

Number Crunch

Starting at the top left with the number provided, work down from one box to another, applying the mathematical instructions to your running total.

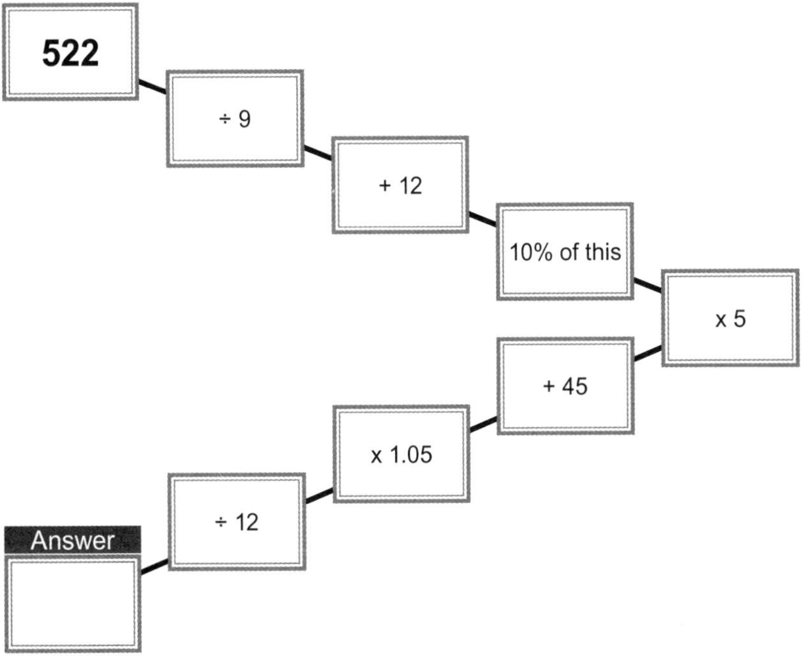

522 → ÷ 9 → + 12 → 10% of this → x 5 → + 45 → x 1.05 → ÷ 12 → Answer

Summing Up

Arrange one of each of the four given numbers, as well as one each of the symbols − (minus), x (times), and + (plus) in every row and column to arrive at the answer at the end of that row or column.

Make the calculations in the order in which they appear: working from left to right, or top to bottom.

Numbers: 3, 4, 7, 8

4	+	7	−	8	x	3	=	9
			x			7	=	27
	x						=	57
				x				
							=	41
=		=		=		=		
28		36		49		32		

9

Isolate

Draw walls to partition the grid into areas (some walls are already drawn in for you). Each area must contain two circles, area sizes must match those shown by the numbers above the grid and each "+" must be linked to at least two walls.

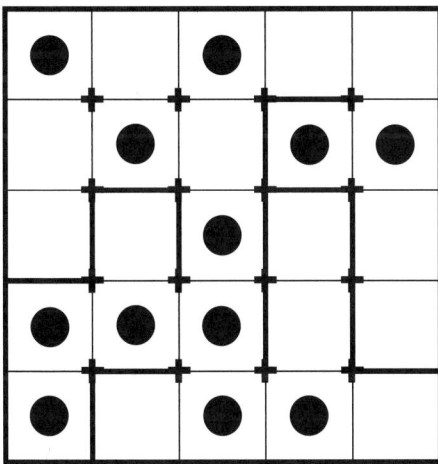

10

Round Up

The number in each circle is the sum of the two numbers below it. Just work out the missing numbers in every circle!

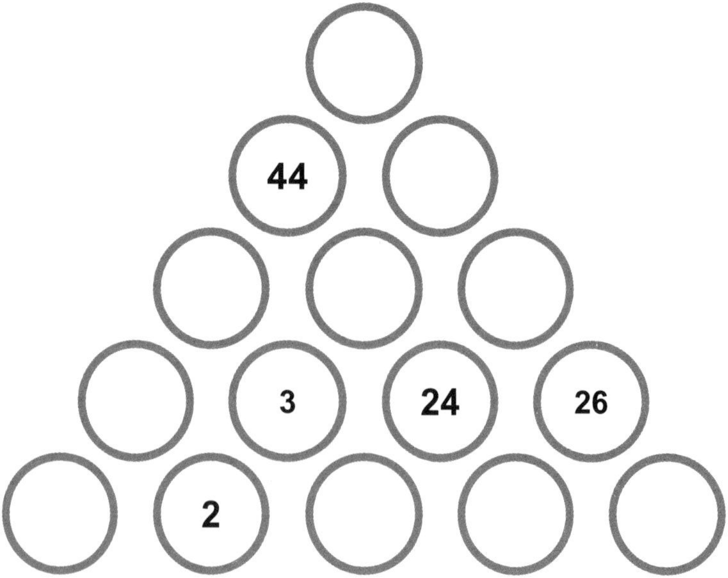

11

One to Nine

Using the numbers below, complete these six equations (three reading across and three reading down). Every number is used once.

Make the calculations in the order in which they appear: working from left to right, or top to bottom.

1 2 3
4 5 6
7 8 9

	−		x		=	16
x		+		−		
	+		x		=	40
+		x		+		
	x	3	−		=	25
=		=		=		
15		33		5		

12

 **MINUTE**

Number Crunch

Starting at the top left with the number provided, work down from one box to another, applying the mathematical instructions to your running total.

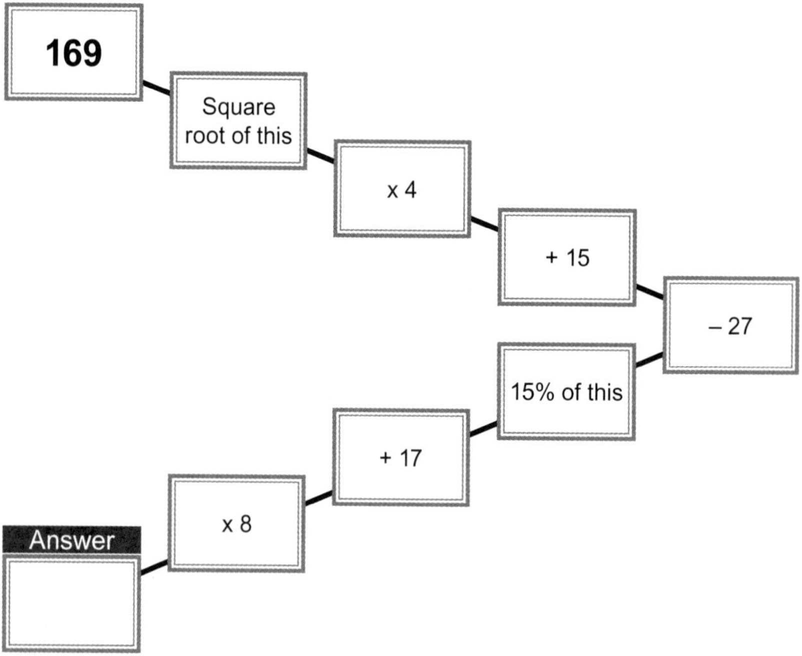

169 → Square root of this → x 4 → + 15 → − 27 → 15% of this → + 17 → x 8 → **Answer**

Summing Up

Arrange one of each of the four given numbers, as well as one each of the symbols – (minus), x (times), and + (plus) in every row and column to arrive at the answer at the end of that row or column.

Make the calculations in the order in which they appear: working from left to right, or top to bottom.

① ⑥
⑧ ⑨

9	–	1	+	8	x	6	=	96
				1			=	5
							=	19
	x						=	11
=		=		=		=		
47		27		69		61		

14

Isolate

Draw walls to partition the grid into areas (some walls are already drawn in for you). Each area must contain two circles, area sizes must match those shown by the numbers above the grid and each "+" must be linked to at least two walls.

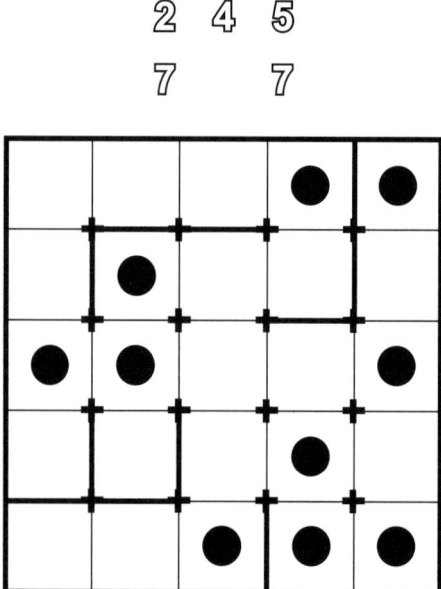

15

Round Up

The number in each circle is the sum of the two numbers below it. Just work out the missing numbers in every circle!

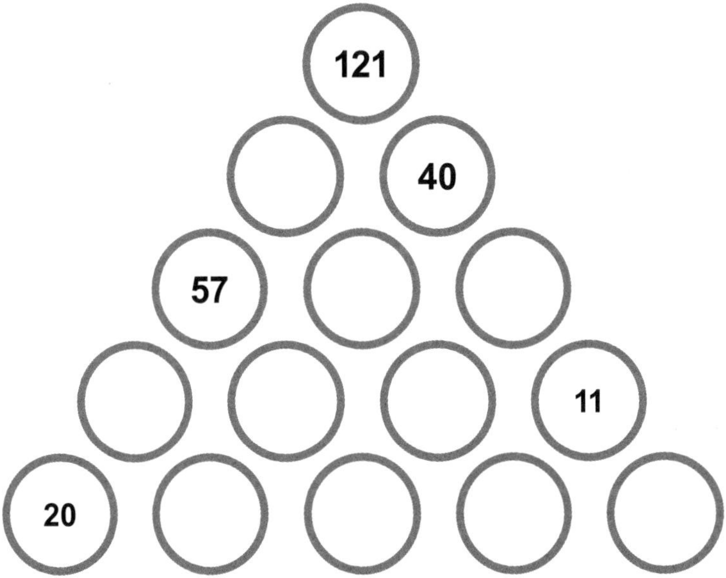

16

One to Nine

Using the numbers below, complete these six equations (three reading across and three reading down). Every number is used once.

Make the calculations in the order in which they appear: working from left to right, or top to bottom.

$$1 \quad 2 \quad 3$$
$$4 \quad 5 \quad 6$$
$$7 \quad 8 \quad 9$$

	x		+		=	10
+		x		−		
	+		x	5	=	70
x		−		x		
	−		+		=	11
=		=		=		
36		6		18		

22

17

Number Crunch

Starting at the top left with the number provided, work down from one box to another, applying the mathematical instructions to your running total.

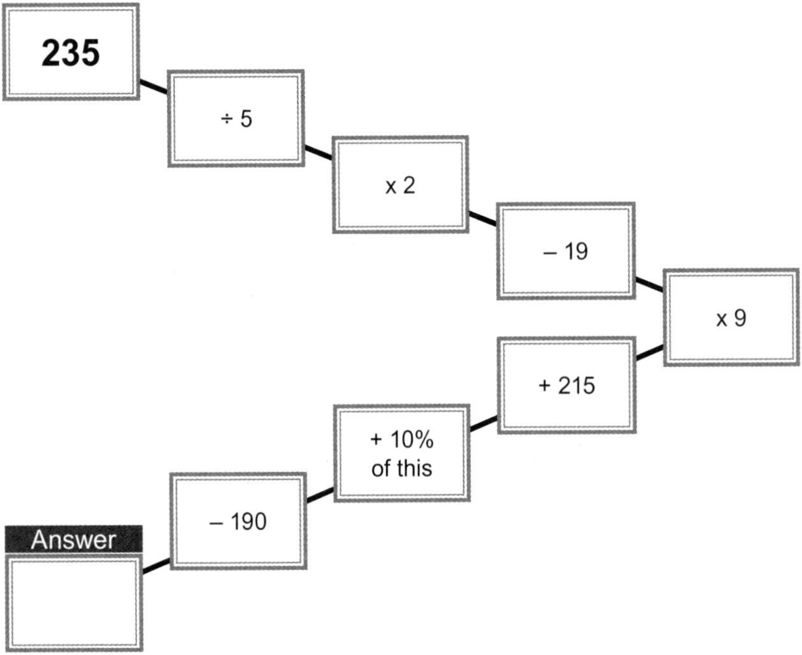

235

÷ 5

x 2

− 19

x 9

+ 215

+ 10% of this

− 190

Answer

18

Summing Up

Arrange one of each of the four given numbers, as well as one each of the symbols – (minus), x (times), and + (plus) in every row and column to arrive at the answer at the end of that row or column.

Make the calculations in the order in which they appear: working from left to right, or top to bottom.

1   6
7   8

7	−	1	+	6	x	8	=	96
x								
							=	97
				1			=	54
							=	9
=		=		=		=		
51		49		35		55		

19

Isolate

Draw walls to partition the grid into areas (some walls are already drawn in for you). Each area must contain two circles, area sizes must match those shown by the numbers above the grid and each "+" must be linked to at least two walls.

2 4 4
4 4 7

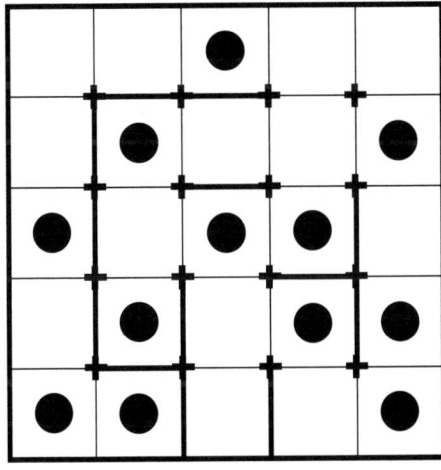

Round Up

The number in each circle is the sum of the two numbers below it. Just work out the missing numbers in every circle!

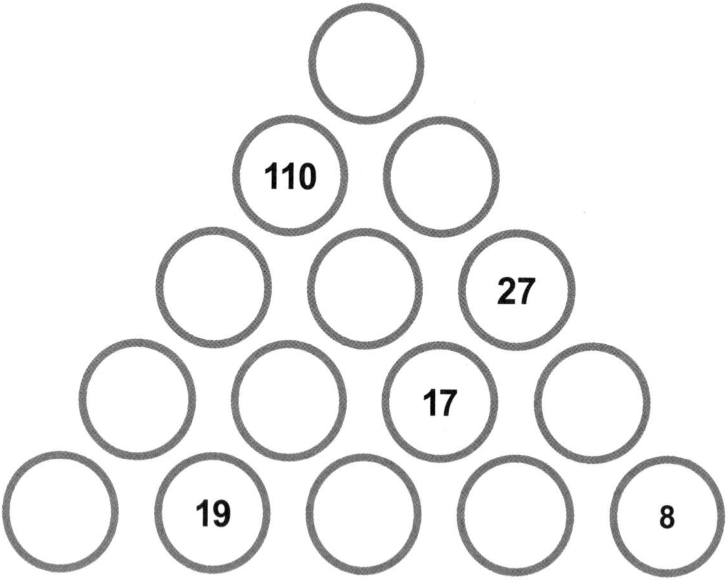

21

One to Nine

Using the numbers below, complete these six equations (three reading across and three reading down). Every number is used once.

Make the calculations in the order in which they appear: working from left to right, or top to bottom.

1 2 3
4 5 6
7 8 9

	x	7	–		=	33
–		+		x		
	+		–		=	7
x		x		+		
	–		x		=	21
=		=		=		
8		16		15		

22

 MINUTE

Number Crunch

Starting at the top left with the number provided, work down from one box to another, applying the mathematical instructions to your running total.

15

2/3 of this

+ 20%

x 14

÷ 3

− 27

x 2

+ 142

Answer

Summing Up

Arrange one of each of the four given numbers, as well as one each of the symbols – (minus), x (times), and + (plus) in every row and column to arrive at the answer at the end of that row or column.

Make the calculations in the order in which they appear: working from left to right, or top to bottom.

2   4
6   8

4	+	8	–	2	x	6	=	60
x								
						=	8
						=	48
	+		8			=	78
=		=		=		=		
10		16		28		46		

24

Isolate

Draw walls to partition the grid into areas (some walls are already drawn in for you). Each area must contain two circles, area sizes must match those shown by the numbers above the grid and each "+" must be linked to at least two walls.

2 4 6
6   7

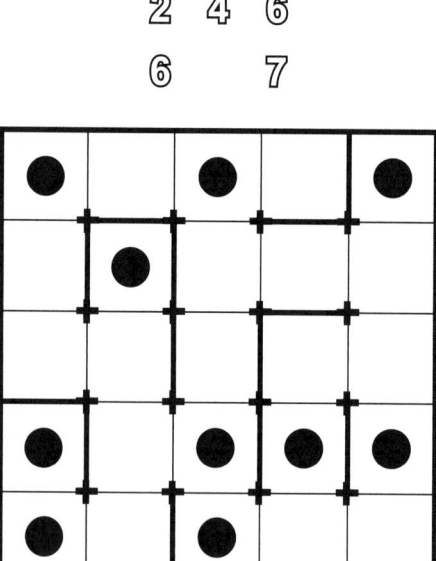

25

Round Up

The number in each circle is the sum of the two numbers below it. Just work out the missing numbers in every circle!

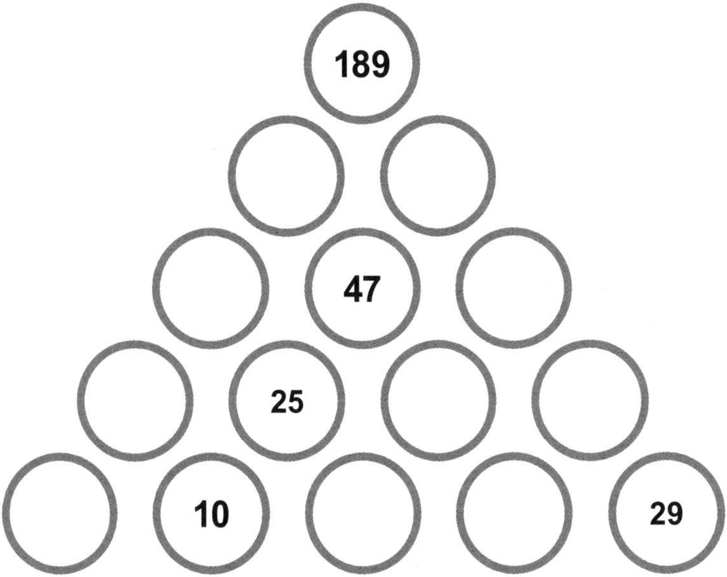

One to Nine

Using the numbers below, complete these six equations (three reading across and three reading down). Every number is used once.

Make the calculations in the order in which they appear: working from left to right, or top to bottom.

1 2 3
4 5 6
7 8 9

6	−		x		=	25
+		+		x		
	x		+		=	16
x		x		−		
	+		x		=	48
=		=		=		
56		45		37		

27

Number Crunch

Starting at the top left with the number provided, work down from one box to another, applying the mathematical instructions to your running total.

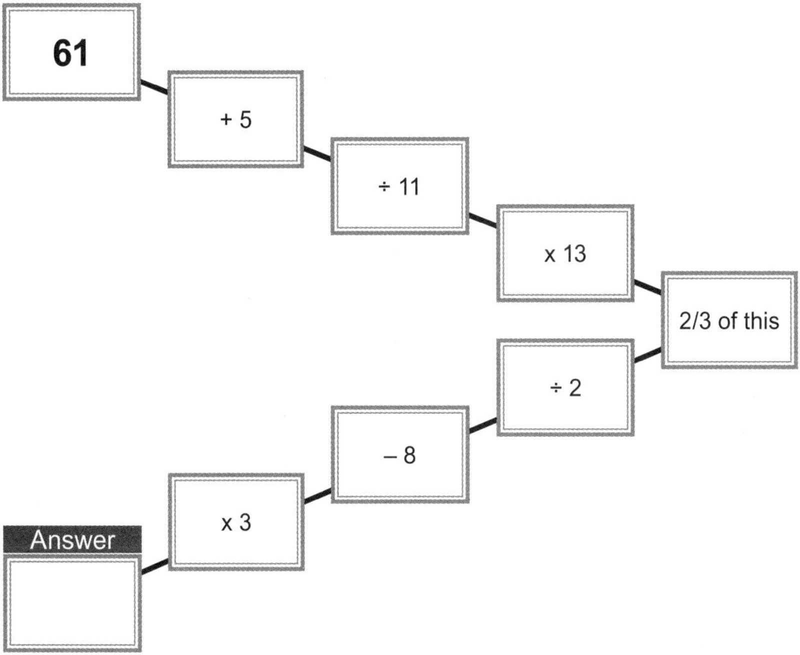

61	→	+ 5	→	÷ 11	→	x 13	→	2/3 of this

Answer	←	x 3	←	− 8	←	÷ 2	←

28

Summing Up

Arrange one of each of the four given numbers, as well as one each of the symbols – (minus), x (times), and + (plus) in every row and column to arrive at the answer at the end of that row or column.

Make the calculations in the order in which they appear: working from left to right, or top to bottom.

4 5
7 8

8	−	4	+	7	x	5	=	55
				−				
							=	40
							=	39
					x		=	49
=		=		=		=		
25		31		29		63		

29

Isolate

Draw walls to partition the grid into areas (some walls are already drawn in for you). Each area must contain two circles, area sizes must match those shown by the numbers above the grid and each "+" must be linked to at least two walls.

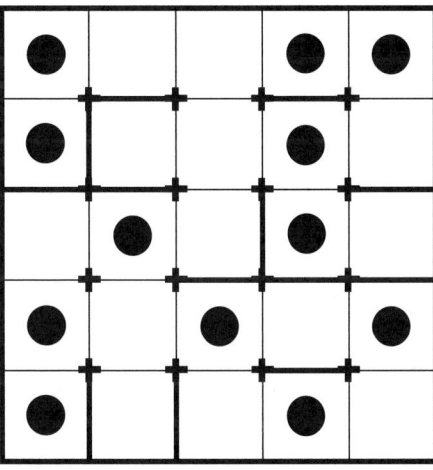

30

Round Up

The number in each circle is the sum of the two numbers below it. Just work out the missing numbers in every circle!

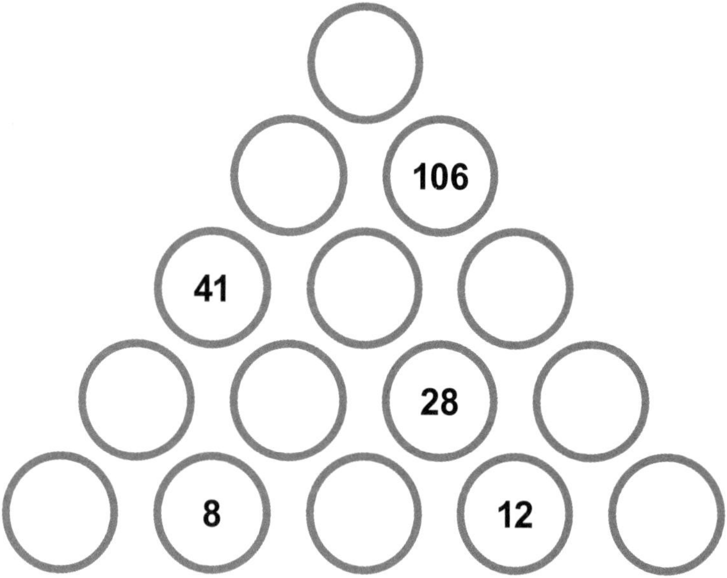

31

One to Nine

Using the numbers below, complete these six equations (three reading across and three reading down). Every number is used once.

Make the calculations in the order in which they appear: working from left to right, or top to bottom.

1 2 3
4 5 6
7 8 9

	x		+		=	14
x		−		+		
	−		x		=	7
+		x		x		
	+		−	2	=	12
=		=		=		
10		48		24		

37

32

Number Crunch

Starting at the top left with the number provided, work down from one box to another, applying the mathematical instructions to your running total.

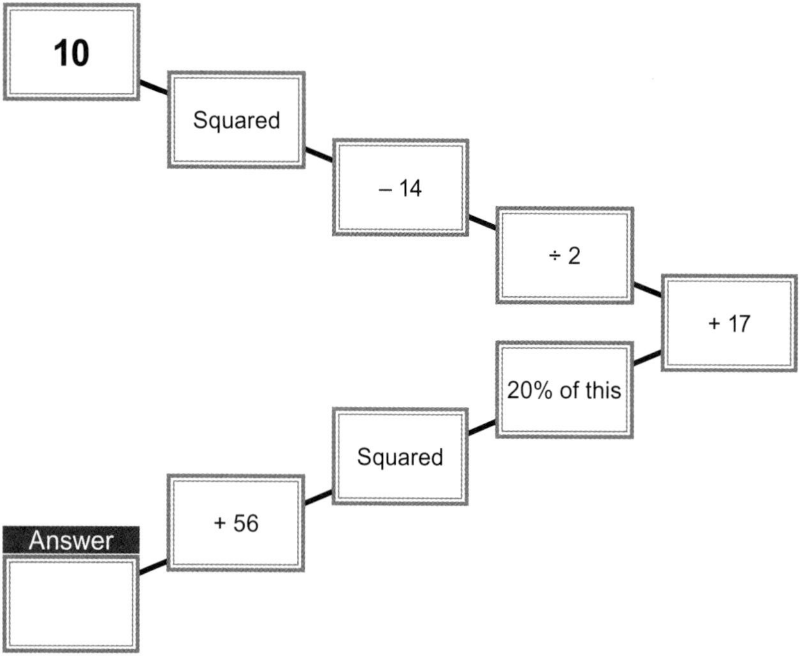

- 10
- Squared
- − 14
- ÷ 2
- + 17
- 20% of this
- Squared
- + 56
- Answer

33

Summing Up

Arrange one of each of the four given numbers, as well as one each of the symbols – (minus), x (times), and + (plus) in every row and column to arrive at the answer at the end of that row or column.

Make the calculations in the order in which they appear: working from left to right, or top to bottom.

3   4
5   9

3	+	5	x	4	–	9	=	23
		–						
						3	=	28
							=	38
				9			=	22
=		=		=		=		
40		12		26		34		

34

Isolate

Draw walls to partition the grid into areas (some walls are already drawn in for you). Each area must contain two circles, area sizes must match those shown by the numbers above the grid and each "+" must be linked to at least two walls.

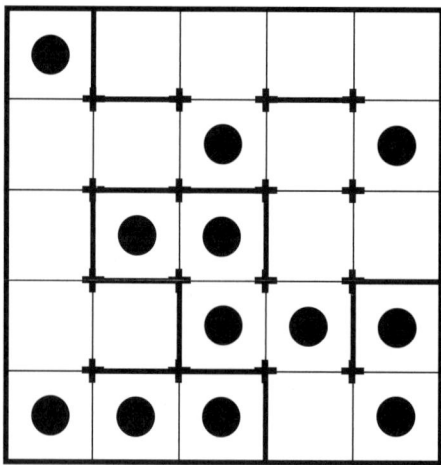

35

MINUTE

Round Up

The number in each circle is the sum of the two numbers below it. Just work out the missing numbers in every circle!

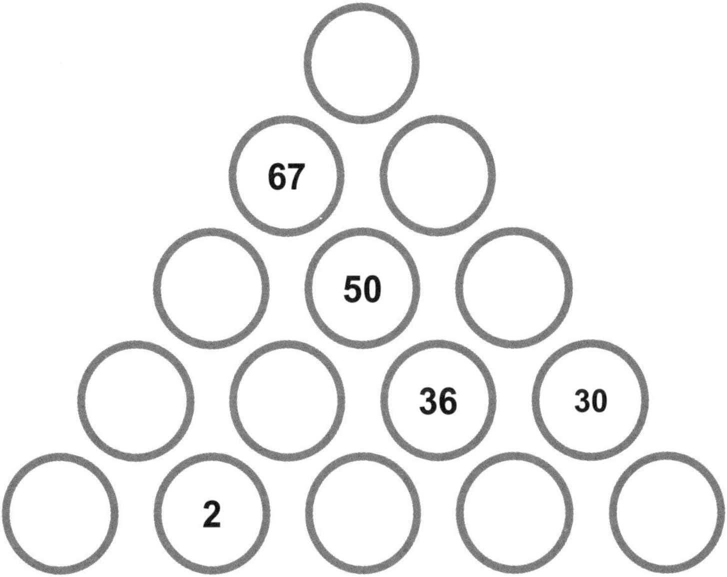

- 67
- 50
- 36
- 30
- 2

36

One to Nine

Using the numbers below, complete these six equations (three reading across and three reading down). Every number is used once.

Make the calculations in the order in which they appear: working from left to right, or top to bottom.

1 2 3
4 5 6
7 8 9

	+		−		=	6
x		−		+		
	x		+		=	8
+		x		−		
9	−		x		=	4
=		=		=		
13		21		7		

37

Number Crunch

Starting at the top left with the number provided, work down from one box to another, applying the mathematical instructions to your running total.

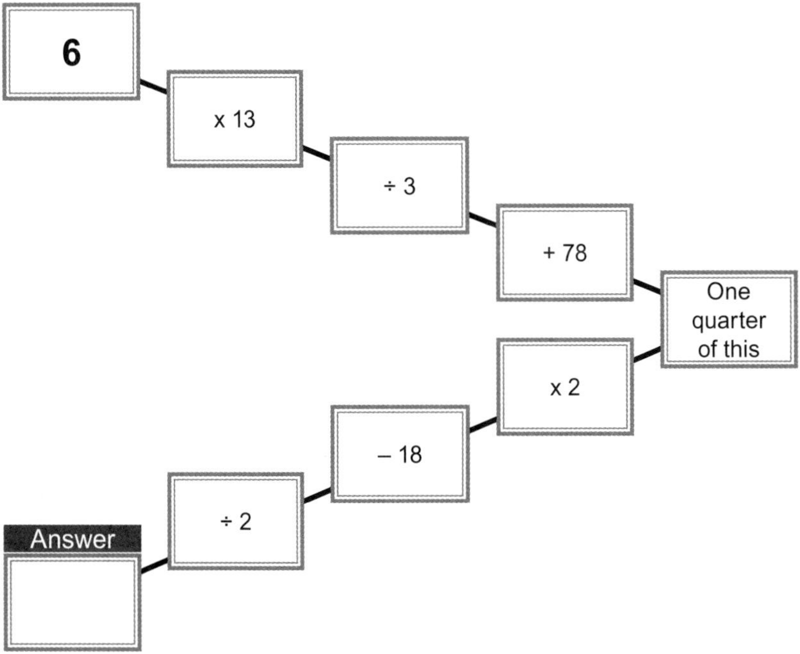

- **6**
- x 13
- ÷ 3
- + 78
- One quarter of this
- x 2
- − 18
- ÷ 2
- Answer

38

Summing Up

Arrange one of each of the four given numbers, as well as one each of the symbols − (minus), x (times), and + (plus) in every row and column to arrive at the answer at the end of that row or column.

Make the calculations in the order in which they appear: working from left to right, or top to bottom.

③ ⑤
⑥ ⑨

5	x	3	−	9	+	6	=	12
						x		
							=	14
		−						
		5					=	27
							=	40
=		=		=		=		
24		36		42		56		

39

Isolate

Draw walls to partition the grid into areas (some walls are already drawn in for you). Each area must contain two circles, area sizes must match those shown by the numbers above the grid and each "+" must be linked to at least two walls.

2 3 4
5 5 6

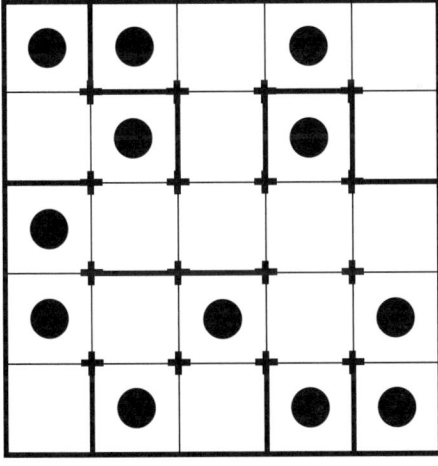

40

Round Up

The number in each circle is the sum of the two numbers below it. Just work out the missing numbers in every circle!

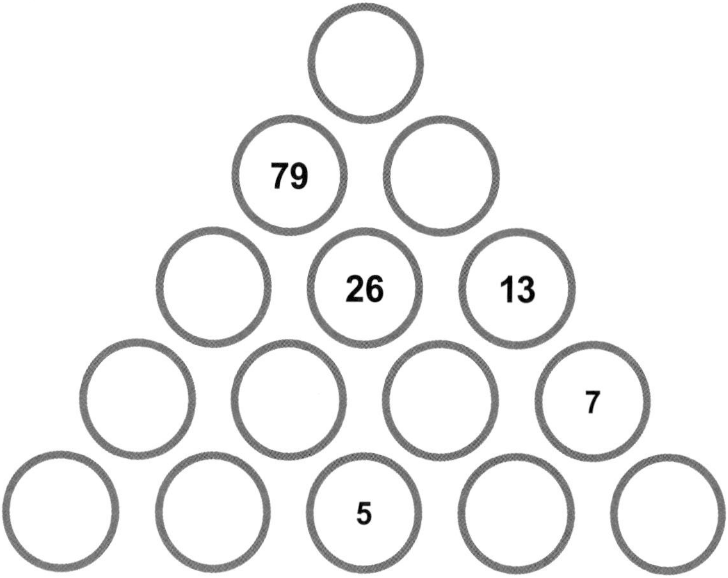

41

One to Nine

Using the numbers below, complete these six equations (three reading across and three reading down). Every number is used once.

Make the calculations in the order in which they appear: working from left to right, or top to bottom.

1 2 3
4 5 6
7 8 9

	+		−		=	12
x		−		+		
3	x		+		=	30
+		x		x		
	−		x		=	16
=		=		=		
21		2		40		

42

Number Crunch

Starting at the top left with the number provided, work down from one box to another, applying the mathematical instructions to your running total.

111 → ÷ 3 → − 12 → Square root of this → x 15 → + 105 → 5% of this → Square root of this → Answer

43

Summing Up

Arrange one of each of the four given numbers, as well as one each of the symbols − (minus), x (times), and + (plus) in every row and column to arrive at the answer at the end of that row or column.

Make the calculations in the order in which they appear: working from left to right, or top to bottom.

2 3
4 9

9	−	2	+	4	x	3	=	33
							=	61
		+		x				
							=	19
						9	=	27
=		=		=		=		
20		14		37		45		

44

Isolate

Draw walls to partition the grid into areas (some walls are already drawn in for you). Each area must contain two circles, area sizes must match those shown by the numbers above the grid and each "+" must be linked to at least two walls.

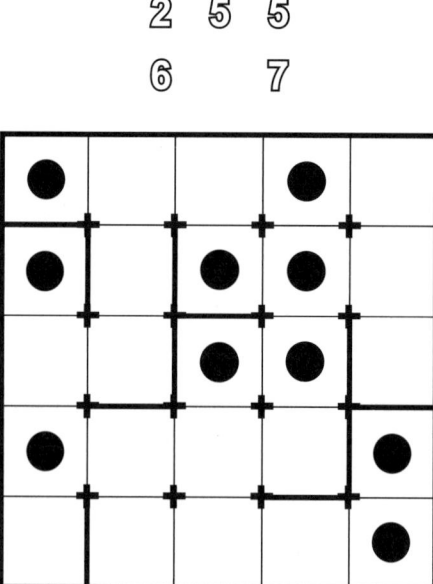

45

Round Up

The number in each circle is the sum of the two numbers below it. Just work out the missing numbers in every circle!

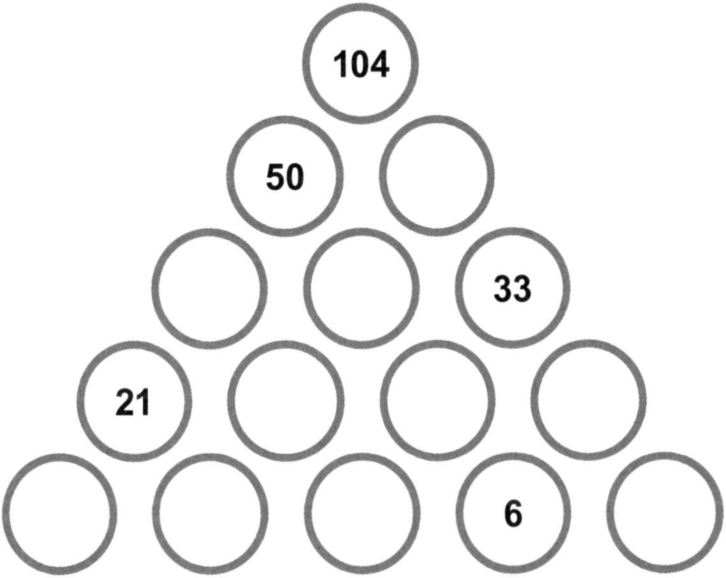

- 104
- 50
- 33
- 21
- 6

46

One to Nine

Using the numbers below, complete these six equations (three reading across and three reading down). Every number is used once.

Make the calculations in the order in which they appear: working from left to right, or top to bottom.

1 2 3
4 5 6
7 8 9

	+		x		=	30
−		−		x		
	x	7	−		=	23
x		x		+		
	x		+		=	11
=		=		=		
2		6		18		

52

47

Number Crunch

Starting at the top left with the number provided, work down from one box to another, applying the mathematical instructions to your running total.

250

50% of this

÷ 5

x 7

x 2

+ 40

x 1.2

÷ 9

Answer

48

Summing Up

Arrange one of each of the four given numbers, as well as one each of the symbols – (minus), x (times), and + (plus) in every row and column to arrive at the answer at the end of that row or column.

Make the calculations in the order in which they appear: working from left to right, or top to bottom.

Numbers: 2, 3, 6, 8

6	+	3	–	8	x	2	=	2
							=	20
		x				+		
							=	36
							=	40
=		=		=		=		
12		16		39		7		

49

Isolate

Draw walls to partition the grid into areas (some walls are already drawn in for you). Each area must contain two circles, area sizes must match those shown by the numbers above the grid and each "+" must be linked to at least two walls.

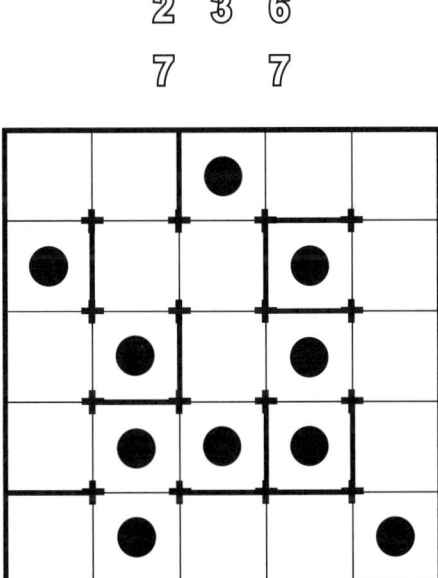

50

Round Up

The number in each circle is the sum of the two numbers below it. Just work out the missing numbers in every circle!

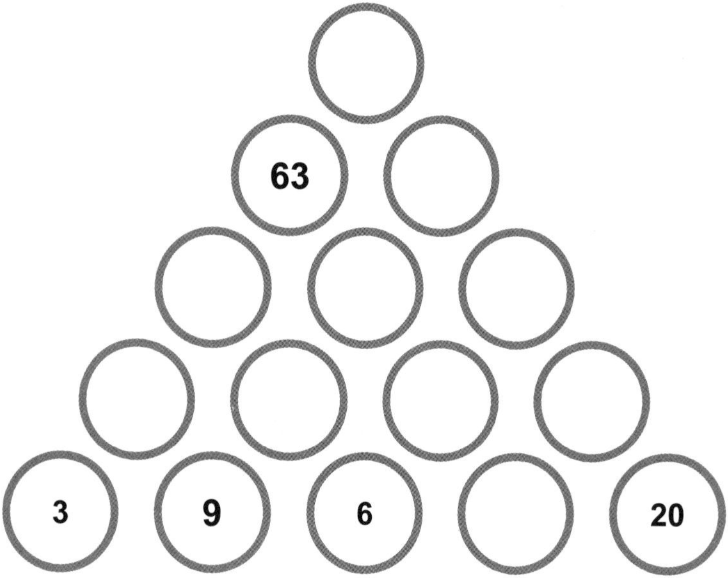

63

3　　**9**　　**6**　　　　**20**

51

One to Nine

Using the numbers below, complete these six equations (three reading across and three reading down). Every number is used once.

Make the calculations in the order in which they appear: working from left to right, or top to bottom.

$$1 \quad 2 \quad 3$$
$$4 \quad 5 \quad 6$$
$$7 \quad 8 \quad 9$$

	−		×		=	4
−		×		+		
	×		+	6	=	30
×		−		×		
	−		×		=	20
=		=		=		
42		38		28		

52

Number Crunch

Starting at the top left with the number provided, work down from one box to another, applying the mathematical instructions to your running total.

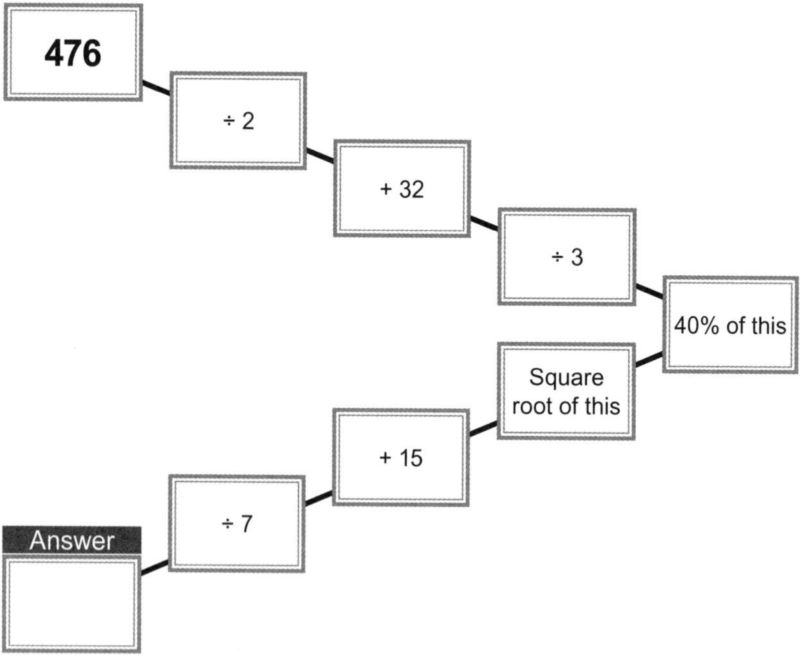

- **476**
- ÷ 2
- + 32
- ÷ 3
- 40% of this
- Square root of this
- + 15
- ÷ 7
- Answer

53

Summing Up

Arrange one of each of the four given numbers, as well as one each of the symbols – (minus), x (times), and + (plus) in every row and column to arrive at the answer at the end of that row or column.

Make the calculations in the order in which they appear: working from left to right, or top to bottom.

3 4
5 8

4	+	8	–	3	x	5	=	45
x								
							=	11
						8	=	19
						x		
							=	29
=		=		=		=		
25		23		39		40		

54

Isolate

Draw walls to partition the grid into areas (some walls are already drawn in for you). Each area must contain two circles, area sizes must match those shown by the numbers above the grid and each "+" must be linked to at least two walls.

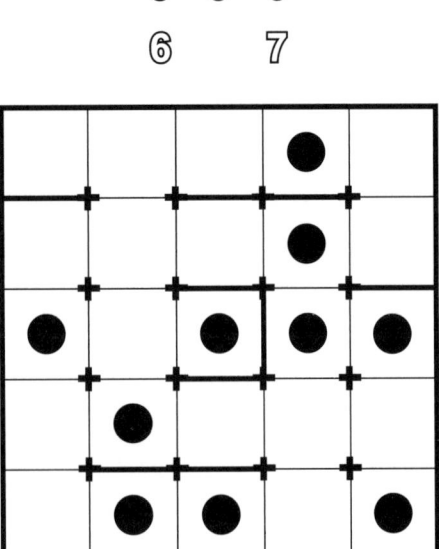

55

Round Up

The number in each circle is the sum of the two numbers below it. Just work out the missing numbers in every circle!

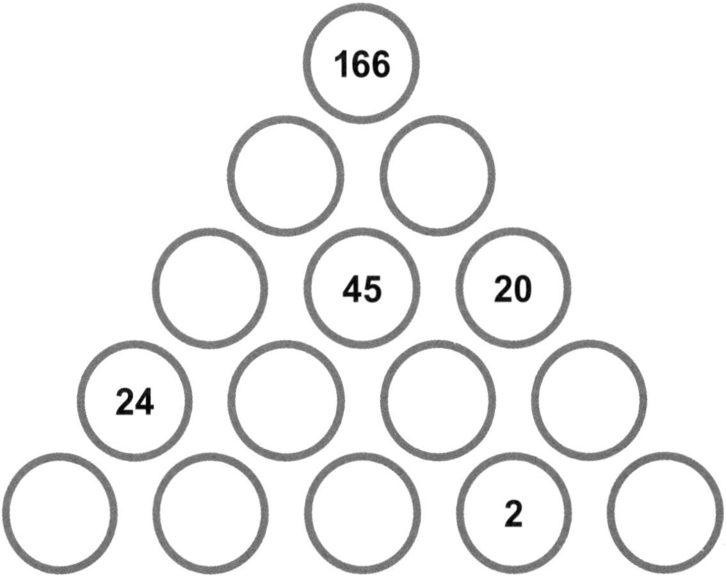

- 166
- 45, 20
- 24
- 2

56

One to Nine

Using the numbers below, complete these six equations (three reading across and three reading down). Every number is used once.

Make the calculations in the order in which they appear: working from left to right, or top to bottom.

1 2 3
4 5 6
7 8 9

4	x	9	−	1	=	35
+		−		x		
7	−	2	x	6	=	30
x		+		−		
5	+	8	−	3	=	10
=		=		=		
55		15		3		

62

Number Crunch

Starting at the top left with the number provided, work down from one box to another, applying the mathematical instructions to your running total.

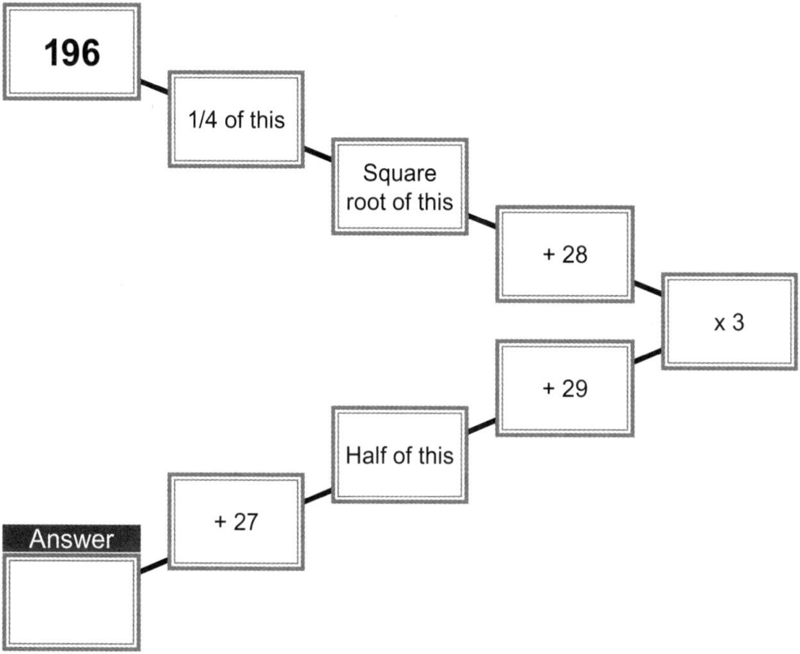

- **196**
- 1/4 of this
- Square root of this
- + 28
- x 3
- + 29
- Half of this
- + 27
- Answer

58

Summing Up

Arrange one of each of the four given numbers, as well as one each of the symbols – (minus), x (times), and + (plus) in every row and column to arrive at the answer at the end of that row or column.

Make the calculations in the order in which they appear: working from left to right, or top to bottom.

2 5
8 9

5	+	9	−	8	x	2	=	12
−								
							=	20
							=	48
						+		
			9				=	59
=		=		=		=		
35		83		17		15		

Isolate

Draw walls to partition the grid into areas (some walls are already drawn in for you). Each area must contain two circles, area sizes must match those shown by the numbers above the grid and each "+" must be linked to at least two walls.

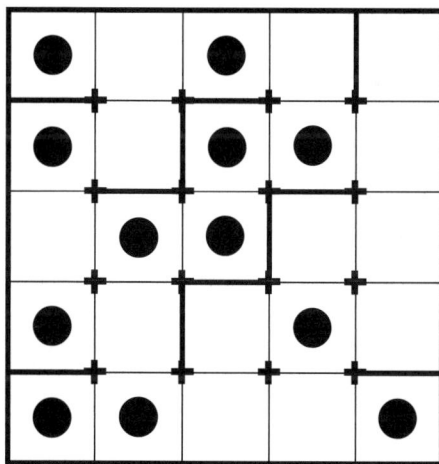

60

Round Up

The number in each circle is the sum of the two numbers below it. Just work out the missing numbers in every circle!

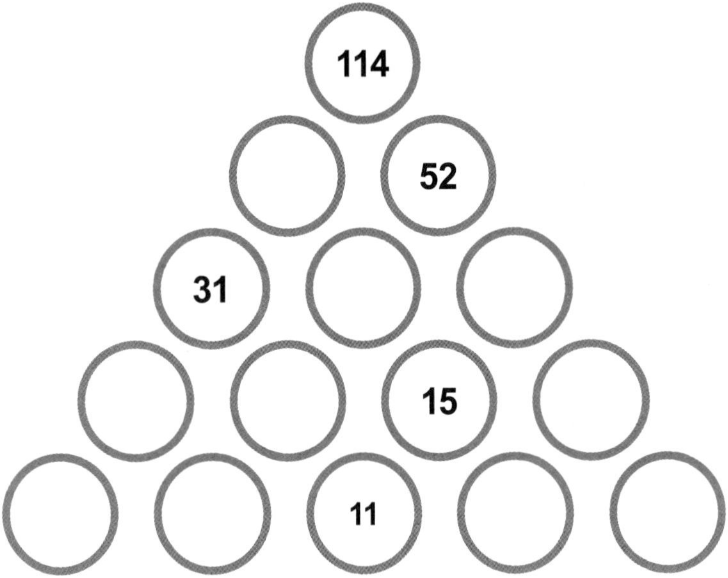

- 114
- __, 52
- 31, __, __
- __, __, 15, __
- __, __, 11, __, __

61

One to Nine

Using the numbers below, complete these six equations (three reading across and three reading down). Every number is used once.

Make the calculations in the order in which they appear: working from left to right, or top to bottom.

$$1 \quad 2 \quad 3$$
$$4 \quad 5 \quad 6$$
$$7 \quad 8 \quad 9$$

	+		−		=	11
x		+		x		
7	−		x		=	25
−		x		+		
	x		−		=	35
=		=		=		
38		90		16		

62

Number Crunch

Starting at the top left with the number provided, work down from one box to another, applying the mathematical instructions to your running total.

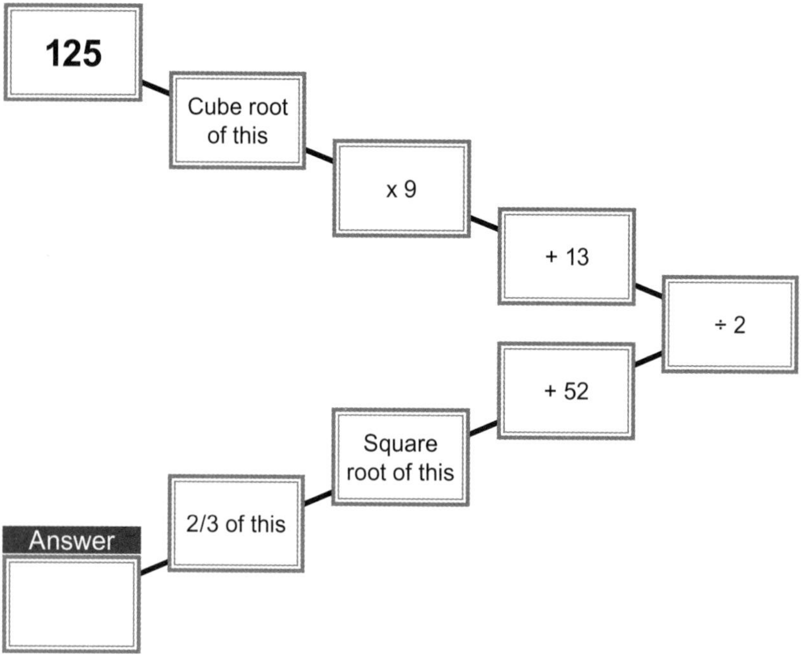

125 → Cube root of this → x 9 → + 13 → ÷ 2 → + 52 → Square root of this → 2/3 of this → Answer

63

Summing Up

Arrange one of each of the four given numbers, as well as one each of the symbols – (minus), x (times), and + (plus) in every row and column to arrive at the answer at the end of that row or column.

Make the calculations in the order in which they appear: working from left to right, or top to bottom.

Numbers: 1, 4, 6, 7

6	–	1	+	7	x	4	=	48
							=	33
	–						=	19
		6	–				=	21
=		=		=		=		
15		9		44		3		

64

Isolate

Draw walls to partition the grid into areas (some walls are already drawn in for you). Each area must contain two circles, area sizes must match those shown by the numbers above the grid and each "+" must be linked to at least two walls.

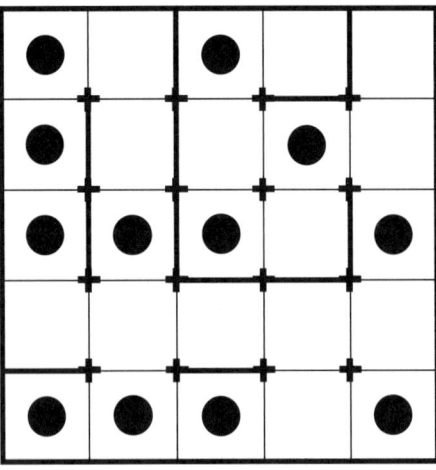

65

Round Up

The number in each circle is the sum of the two numbers below it. Just work out the missing numbers in every circle!

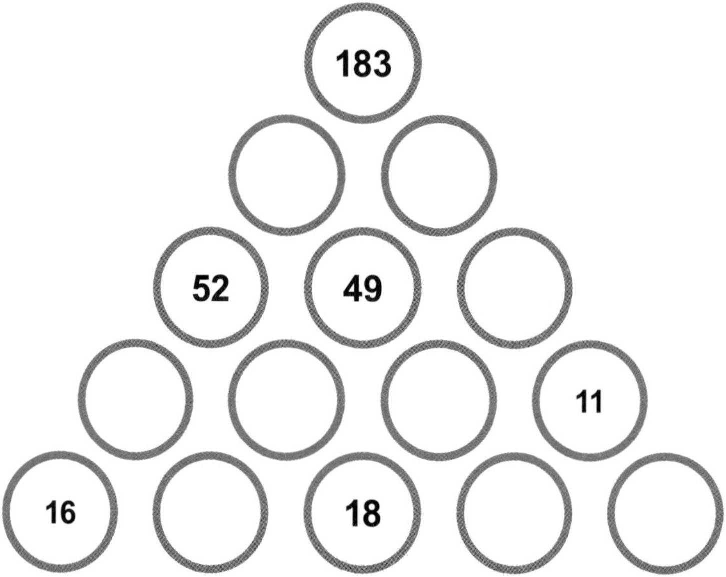

```
            (183)
         (  )  (  )
      (52) (49) (  )
    (  ) (  ) (  ) (11)
 (16) (  ) (18) (  ) (  )
```

66

One to Nine

Using the numbers below, complete these six equations (three reading across and three reading down). Every number is used once.

Make the calculations in the order in which they appear: working from left to right, or top to bottom.

$$1 \quad 2 \quad 3$$
$$4 \quad 5 \quad 6$$
$$7 \quad 8 \quad 9$$

	−		+		=	14
−		+		x		
	x	3	−		=	7
x		x		−		
	+		x		=	36
=		=		=		
28		8		44		

1 MINUTE

67

Number Crunch

Starting at the top left with the number provided, work down from one box to another, applying the mathematical instructions to your running total.

87

+ 9

÷ 12

+ 12

Plus 5% of this

÷ 7

x 19

+ 73

Answer

68

Summing Up

Arrange one of each of the four given numbers, as well as one each of the symbols – (minus), x (times), and + (plus) in every row and column to arrive at the answer at the end of that row or column.

Make the calculations in the order in which they appear: working from left to right, or top to bottom.

5   6

8   9

5	+	9	x	6	–	8	=	76
				x		+		
			x				=	17
–								
		8	+				=	36
			–			5	=	25
=		=		=		=		
16		38		44		55		

69

Isolate

Draw walls to partition the grid into areas (some walls are already drawn in for you). Each area must contain two circles, area sizes must match those shown by the numbers above the grid and each "+" must be linked to at least two walls.

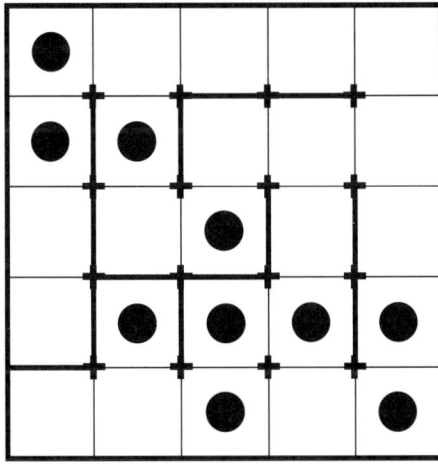

70

Round Up

The number in each circle is the sum of the two numbers below it. Just work out the missing numbers in every circle!

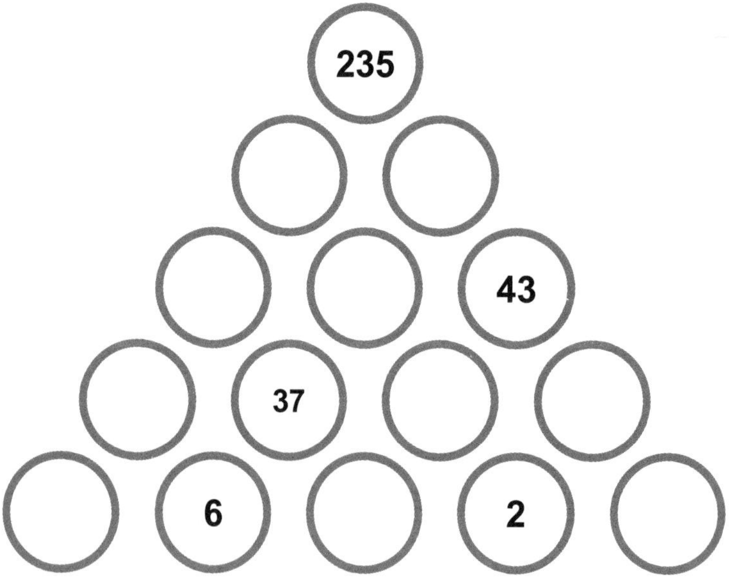

Pyramid values (top to bottom):
- Row 1: 235
- Row 2: _, _
- Row 3: _, _, 43
- Row 4: _, 37, _, _
- Row 5: _, 6, _, 2, _

71

One to Nine

Using the numbers below, complete these six equations (three reading across and three reading down). Every number is used once.

Make the calculations in the order in which they appear: working from left to right, or top to bottom.

1 2 3
4 5 6
7 8 9

	+	9	−		=	10
−		+		x		
	x		+		=	15
x		x		+		
	+		x		=	72
=		=		=		
9		96		12		

72

 MINUTE

Number Crunch

Starting at the top left with the number provided, work down from one box to another, applying the mathematical instructions to your running total.

13 → Squared → + 31 → One quarter of this → x 5 → + 25 → − 125 → One third of this → **Answer**

73

Summing Up

Arrange one of each of the four given numbers, as well as one each of the symbols – (minus), x (times), and + (plus) in every row and column to arrive at the answer at the end of that row or column.

Make the calculations in the order in which they appear: working from left to right, or top to bottom.

①　③
⑥　⑦

7	–	1	+	3	x	6	=	54
						–		
			x				=	62
x								
				6			=	10
	–	3	+				=	28
=		=		=		=		
4		46		16		56		

79

74

Isolate

Draw walls to partition the grid into areas (some walls are already drawn in for you). Each area must contain two circles, area sizes must match those shown by the numbers above the grid and each "+" must be linked to at least two walls.

3 4 4
4 4 6

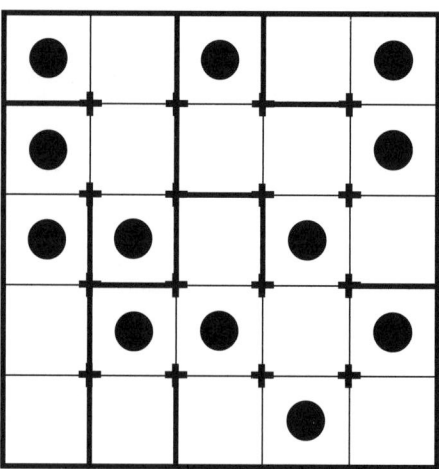

75

Round Up

The number in each circle is the sum of the two numbers below it. Just work out the missing numbers in every circle!

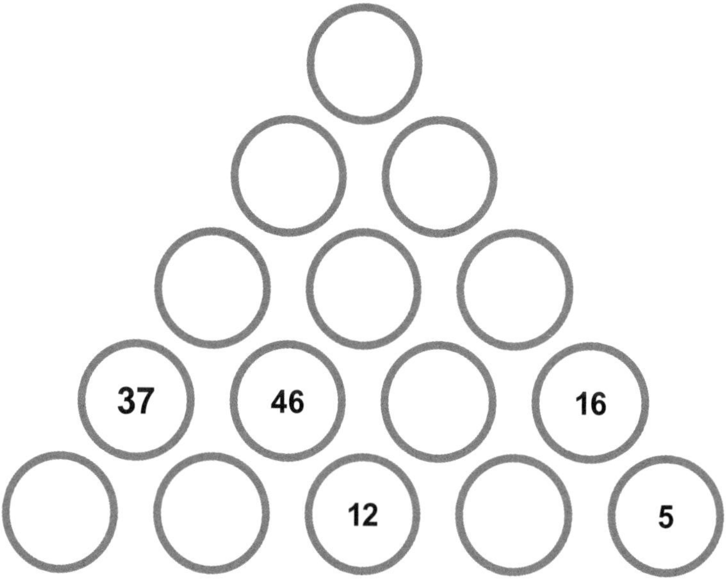

76

One to Nine

Using the numbers below, complete these six equations (three reading across and three reading down). Every number is used once.

Make the calculations in the order in which they appear: working from left to right, or top to bottom.

1 2 3
4 5 6
7 8 9

4	+		x		=	12
−		x		+		
	x		−		=	7
x		−		x		
	−		+		=	8
=		=		=		
18		33		24		

82

77

Number Crunch

Starting at the top left with the number provided, work down from one box to another, applying the mathematical instructions to your running total.

- **75**
- x 7
- ÷ 25
- ÷ 7
- x 16
- One sixth of this
- ÷ 4
- x 98

Answer

78

Summing Up

Arrange one of each of the four given numbers, as well as one each of the symbols – (minus), x (times), and + (plus) in every row and column to arrive at the answer at the end of that row or column.

Make the calculations in the order in which they appear: working from left to right, or top to bottom.

2   3
7   9

7	+	9	–	2	x	3	=	42
				+				
	x						=	20
						–		
			x				=	44
				9			=	38
=		=		=		=		
48		10		26		32		

79

Isolate

Draw walls to partition the grid into areas (some walls are already drawn in for you). Each area must contain two circles, area sizes must match those shown by the numbers above the grid and each "+" must be linked to at least two walls.

3 3 4
4 5 6

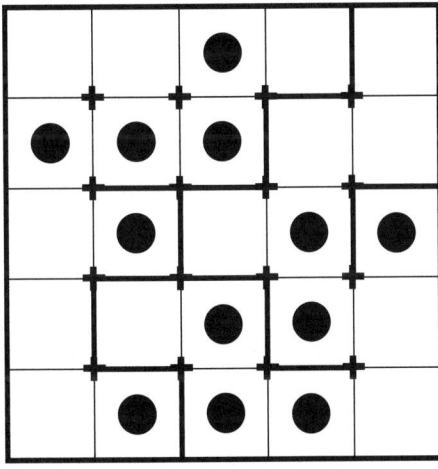

80

Round Up

The number in each circle is the sum of the two numbers below it. Just work out the missing numbers in every circle!

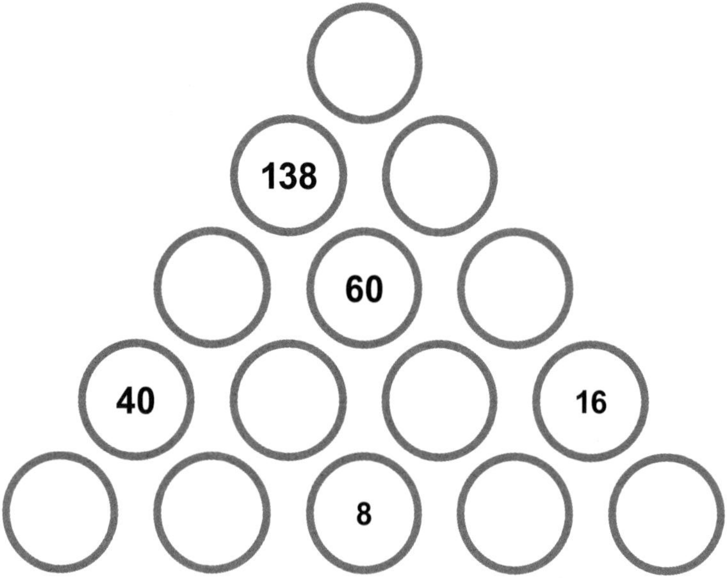

81

One to Nine

Using the numbers below, complete these six equations (three reading across and three reading down). Every number is used once.

Make the calculations in the order in which they appear: working from left to right, or top to bottom.

1 2 3
4 5 6
7 8 9

	+		x		=	30
−		x		+		
	x		−	5	=	3
x		+		x		
	−		x		=	35
=		=		=		
18		20		77		

82

Number Crunch

Starting at the top left with the number provided, work down from one box to another, applying the mathematical instructions to your running total.

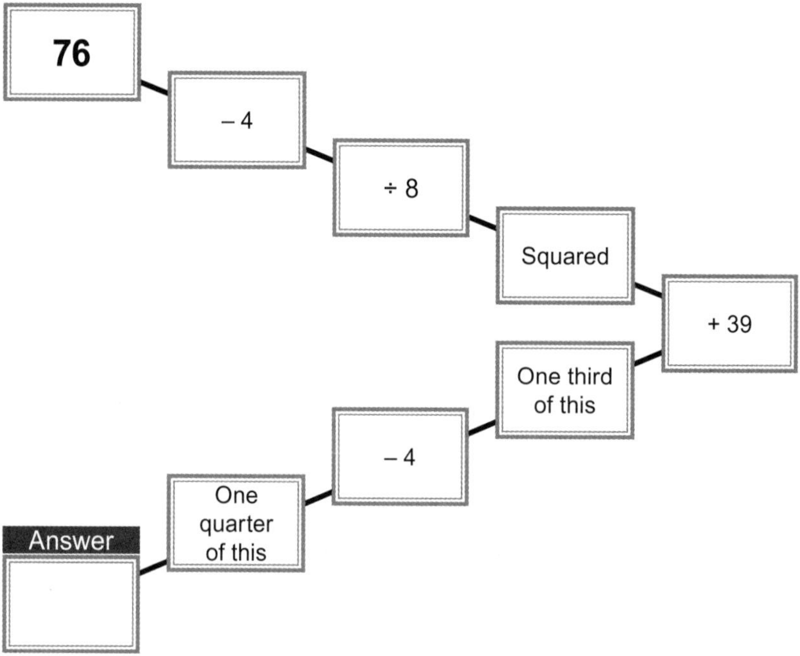

76 → − 4 → ÷ 8 → Squared → + 39 → One third of this → − 4 → One quarter of this → **Answer**

83

Summing Up

Arrange one of each of the four given numbers, as well as one each of the symbols – (minus), x (times), and + (plus) in every row and column to arrive at the answer at the end of that row or column.

Make the calculations in the order in which they appear: working from left to right, or top to bottom.

Numbers: 1, 5, 6, 8

5	+	8	−	1	x	6	=	72
1			+				=	3
		6	x				=	11
+						+		
							=	65
=		=		=		=		
38		35		27		52		

84

Isolate

Draw walls to partition the grid into areas (some walls are already drawn in for you). Each area must contain two circles, area sizes must match those shown by the numbers above the grid and each "+" must be linked to at least two walls.

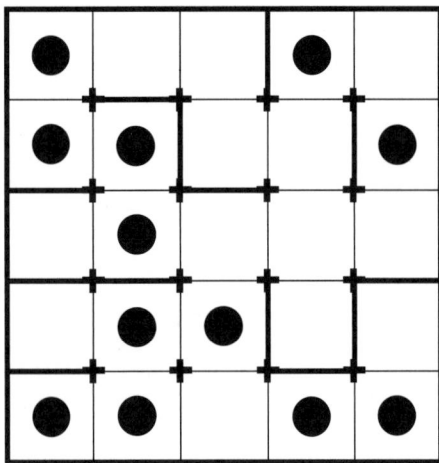

85

Round Up

The number in each circle is the sum of the two numbers below it. Just work out the missing numbers in every circle!

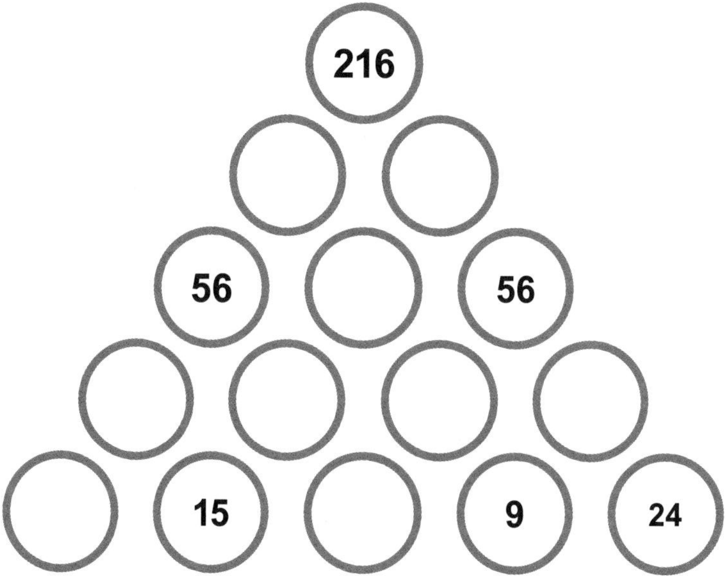

- 216
- ( ) ( )
- 56 ( ) 56
- ( ) ( ) ( ) ( )
- ( ) 15 ( ) 9 24

86

One to Nine

Using the numbers below, complete these six equations (three reading across and three reading down). Every number is used once.

Make the calculations in the order in which they appear: working from left to right, or top to bottom.

$$1 \quad 2 \quad 3$$
$$4 \quad 5 \quad 6$$
$$7 \quad 8 \quad 9$$

	−		x		=	12
+		x		+		
8	x		−		=	41
x		−		x		
	−		x		=	18
=		=		=		
52		4		90		

Number Crunch

Starting at the top left with the number provided, work down from one box to another, applying the mathematical instructions to your running total.

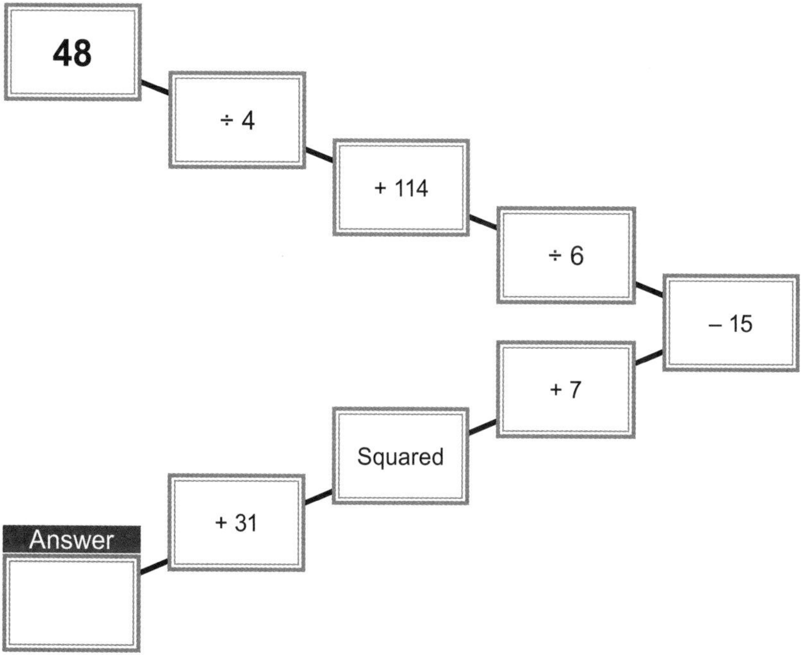

- 48
- ÷ 4
- + 114
- ÷ 6
- − 15
- + 7
- Squared
- + 31
- Answer

88

Summing Up

Arrange one of each of the four given numbers, as well as one each of the symbols – (minus), x (times), and + (plus) in every row and column to arrive at the answer at the end of that row or column.

Make the calculations in the order in which they appear: working from left to right, or top to bottom.

4   5
6   8

4	x	6	–	8	+	5	=	21
+								
		x				6	=	18
				5	x		=	36
		+						
	–						=	14
=		=		=		=		
30		12		26		34		

89

Isolate

Draw walls to partition the grid into areas (some walls are already drawn in for you). Each area must contain two circles, area sizes must match those shown by the numbers above the grid and each "+" must be linked to at least two walls.

2 3 4
4 5 7

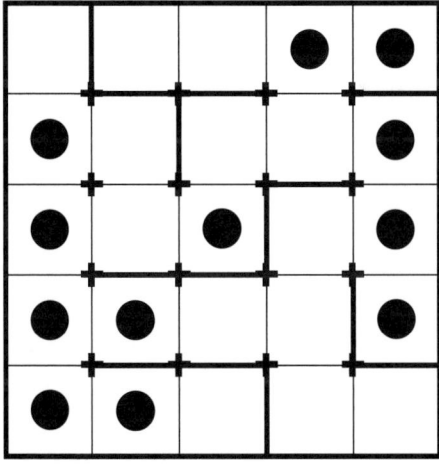

1 MINUTE

90

Round Up

The number in each circle is the sum of the two numbers below it. Just work out the missing numbers in every circle!

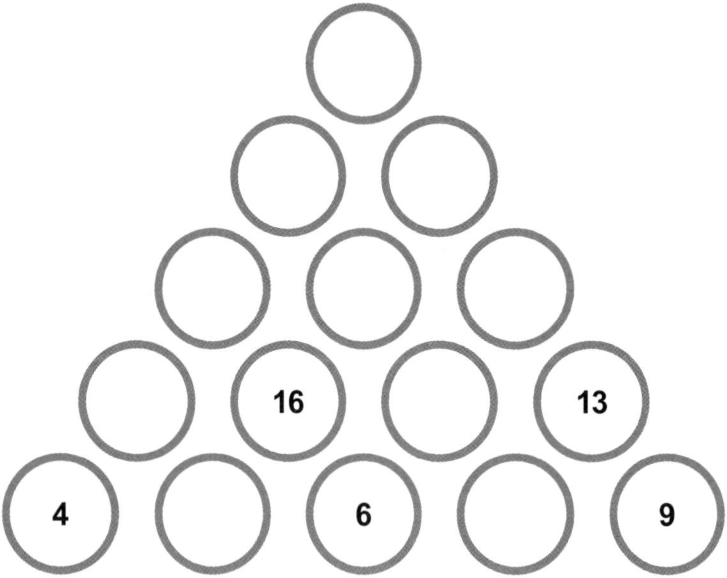

91

One to Nine

Using the numbers below, complete these six equations (three reading across and three reading down). Every number is used once.

Make the calculations in the order in which they appear: working from left to right, or top to bottom.

$$1 \quad 2 \quad 3$$
$$4 \quad 5 \quad 6$$
$$7 \quad 8 \quad 9$$

	+	2	x		=	30
+		x		−		
	+		−		=	12
−		+		x		
	−		x		=	49
=		=		=		
2		19		14		

1 MINUTE

92

Number Crunch

Starting at the top left with the number provided, work down from one box to another, applying the mathematical instructions to your running total.

47

– 38

Squared

÷ 3

+ 1/3 of this

Square root of this

x 7

– 18

Answer

93

Summing Up

Arrange one of each of the four given numbers, as well as one each of the symbols – (minus), x (times), and + (plus) in every row and column to arrive at the answer at the end of that row or column.

Make the calculations in the order in which they appear: working from left to right, or top to bottom.

2   3
5   7

3	x	7	−	5	+	2	=	18
							=	24
x								
			x			7	=	14
				+				
							=	15
=		=		=		=		
9		28		34		30		

94

Isolate

Draw walls to partition the grid into areas (some walls are already drawn in for you). Each area must contain two circles, area sizes must match those shown by the numbers above the grid and each "+" must be linked to at least two walls.

3 3 4
5 5 5

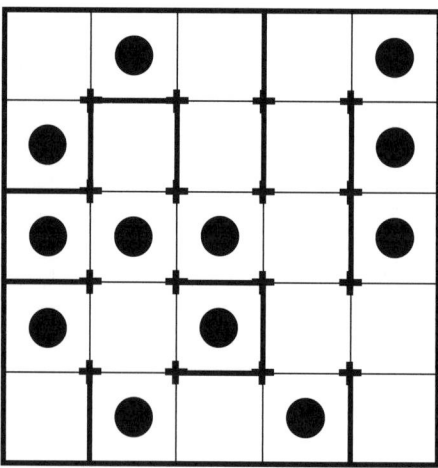

95

Round Up

The number in each circle is the sum of the two numbers below it. Just work out the missing numbers in every circle!

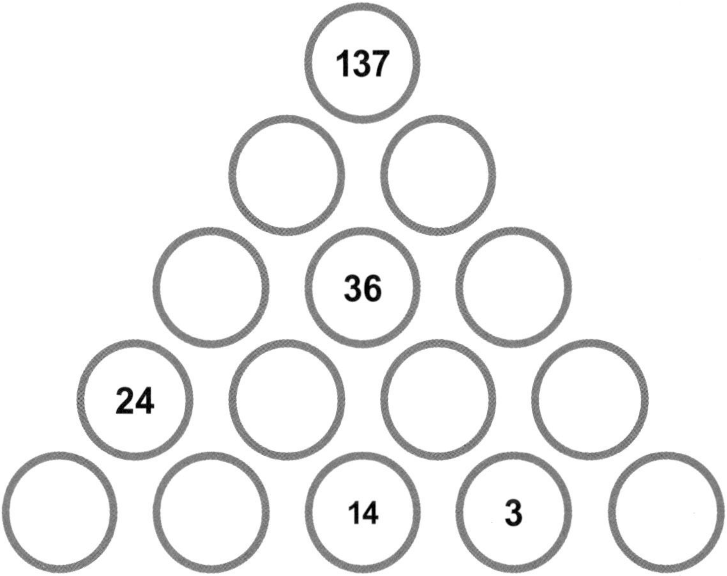

96

One to Nine

Using the numbers below, complete these six equations (three reading across and three reading down). Every number is used once.

Make the calculations in the order in which they appear: working from left to right, or top to bottom.

1 2 3
4 5 6
7 8 9

	−		+		=	14
−		+		−		
4	+		−		=	9
×		×		+		
	×		+		=	11
=		=		=		
5		60		9		

102

97

Number Crunch

Starting at the top left with the number provided, work down from one box to another, applying the mathematical instructions to your running total.

- **10**
- 2/5 of this
- Squared
- 3/4 of this
- x 9
- ÷ 6
- + 48
- ÷ 3
- Answer

98

Summing Up

Arrange one of each of the four given numbers, as well as one each of the symbols – (minus), x (times), and + (plus) in every row and column to arrive at the answer at the end of that row or column.

Make the calculations in the order in which they appear: working from left to right, or top to bottom.

2 3

7 8

3	+	8	x	2	–	7	=	15
						+		
							=	48
		+						
							=	24
		2					=	12
=		=		=		=		
64		8		33		27		

99

Isolate

Draw walls to partition the grid into areas (some walls are already drawn in for you). Each area must contain two circles, area sizes must match those shown by the numbers above the grid and each "+" must be linked to at least two walls.

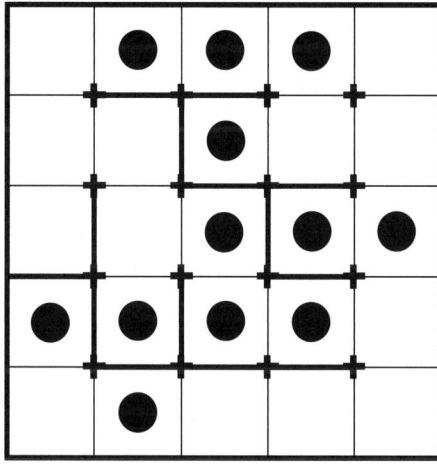

100

Round Up

The number in each circle is the sum of the two numbers below it. Just work out the missing numbers in every circle!

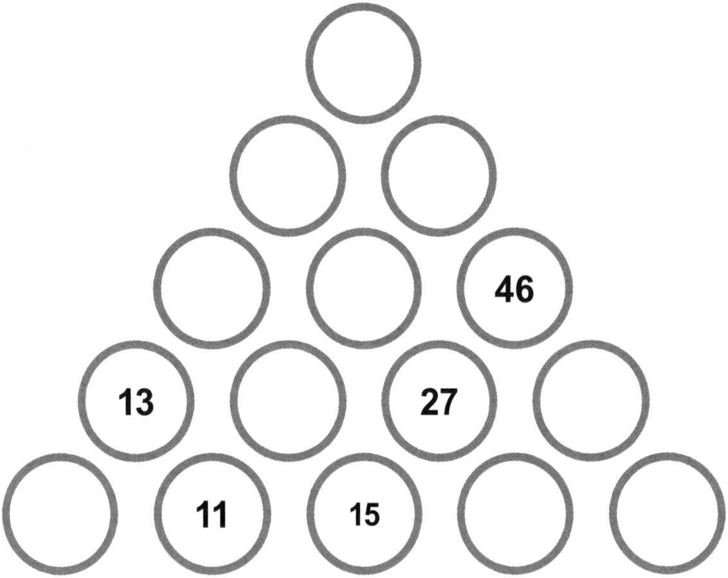

101

One to Nine

Using the numbers below, complete these six equations (three reading across and three reading down). Every number is used once.

Make the calculations in the order in which they appear: working from left to right, or top to bottom.

$$1 \quad 2 \quad 3$$
$$4 \quad 5 \quad 6$$
$$7 \quad 8 \quad 9$$

	x		−		=	30
x		+		−		
3	+		x		=	10
+		−		+		
	−		x		=	6
=		=		=		
20		11		7		

1 MINUTE

102

Number Crunch

Starting at the top left with the number provided, work down from one box to another, applying the mathematical instructions to your running total.

94

– 16

÷ 2

2/3 of this

+ 14

3/5 of this

x 3

+ 28

Answer

103

Summing Up

Arrange one of each of the four given numbers, as well as one each of the symbols – (minus), x (times), and + (plus) in every row and column to arrive at the answer at the end of that row or column.

Make the calculations in the order in which they appear: working from left to right, or top to bottom.

③ ⑥

⑦ ⑨

3	+	7	–	9	x	6	=	6
x								
							=	43
				–				
							=	58
7				3	x		=	36
=		=		=		=		
26		42		24		48		

104

Isolate

Draw walls to partition the grid into areas (some walls are already drawn in for you). Each area must contain two circles, area sizes must match those shown by the numbers above the grid and each "+" must be linked to at least two walls.

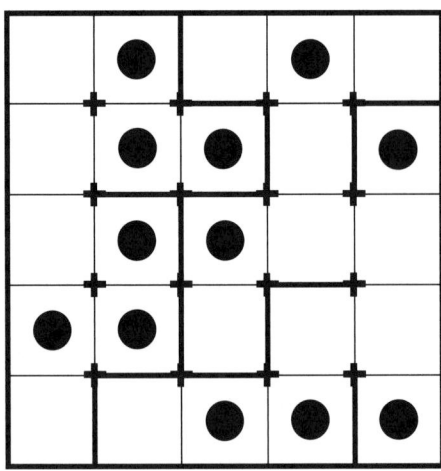

105

Round Up

The number in each circle is the sum of the two numbers below it. Just work out the missing numbers in every circle!

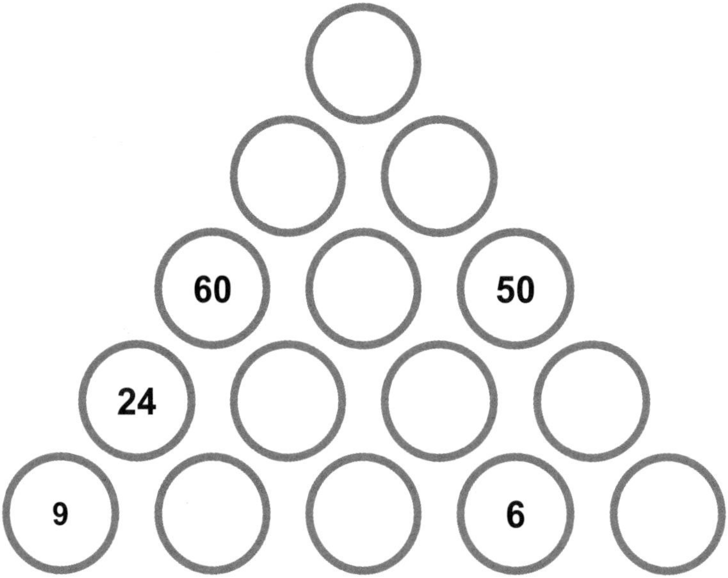

60   50

24

9   6

106

One to Nine

Using the numbers below, complete these six equations (three reading across and three reading down). Every number is used once.

Make the calculations in the order in which they appear: working from left to right, or top to bottom.

1 2 3
4 5 6
7 8 9

3	+	7	x	1	=	10
x		−		+		
6	−	5	x	9	=	9
+		x		x		
8	x	4	+	2	=	34
=		=		=		
26		8		20		

107

Number Crunch

Starting at the top left with the number provided, work down from one box to another, applying the mathematical instructions to your running total.

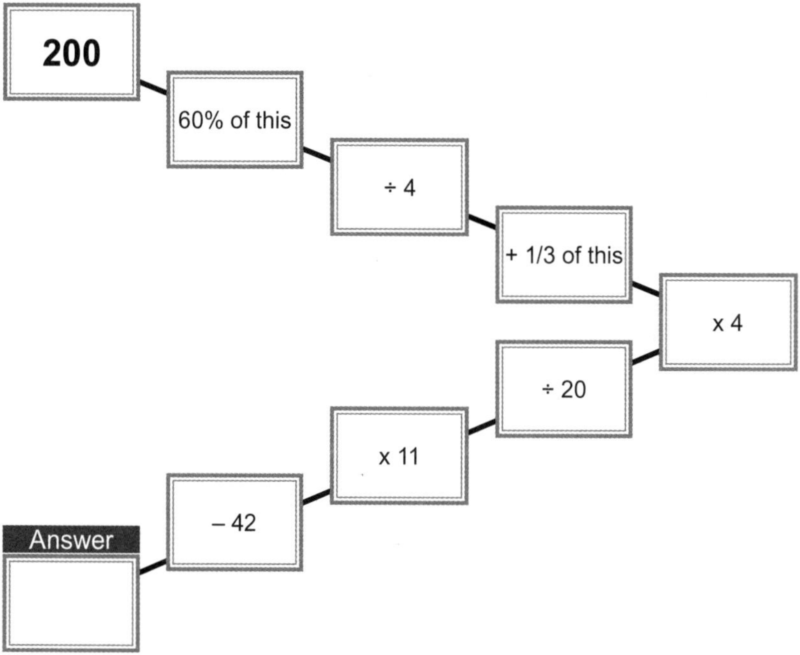

200 → 60% of this → ÷ 4 → + 1/3 of this → x 4 → ÷ 20 → x 11 → − 42 → Answer

108

Summing Up

Arrange one of each of the four given numbers, as well as one each of the symbols – (minus), x (times), and + (plus) in every row and column to arrive at the answer at the end of that row or column.

Make the calculations in the order in which they appear: working from left to right, or top to bottom.

Numbers: 3, 5, 6, 9

5	+	9	x	3	–	6	=	36
	x			6			=	18
9							=	72
							=	32
=		=		=		=		
24		42		14		40		

109

Isolate

Draw walls to partition the grid into areas (some walls are already drawn in for you). Each area must contain two circles, area sizes must match those shown by the numbers above the grid and each "+" must be linked to at least two walls.

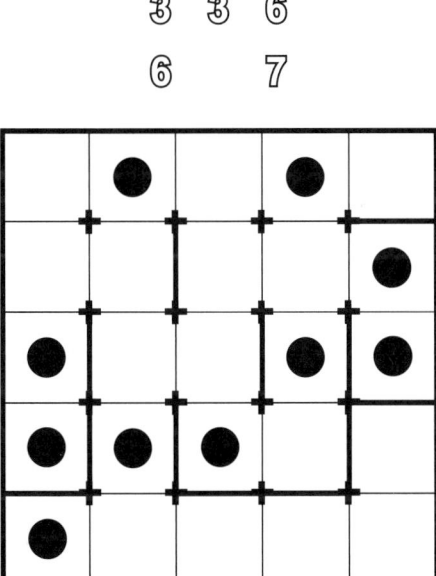

Round Up

The number in each circle is the sum of the two numbers below it. Just work out the missing numbers in every circle!

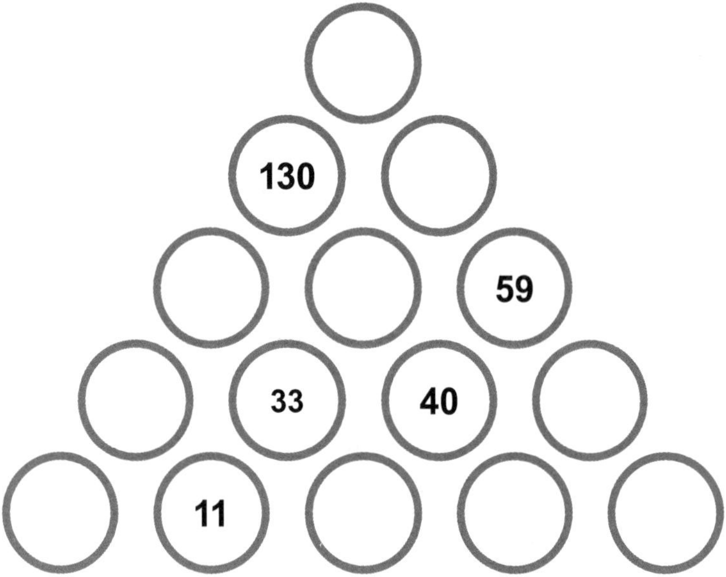

111

One to Nine

Using the numbers below, complete these six equations (three reading across and three reading down). Every number is used once.

Make the calculations in the order in which they appear: working from left to right, or top to bottom.

$$1\ \ 2\ \ 3$$
$$4\ \ 5\ \ 6$$
$$7\ \ 8\ \ 9$$

	x		−	9	=	9
+		−		+		
	+		x		=	49
x		x		x		
	−		+		=	11
=		=		=		
40		1		64		

117

1 MINUTE

112

Number Crunch

Starting at the top left with the number provided, work down from one box to another, applying the mathematical instructions to your running total.

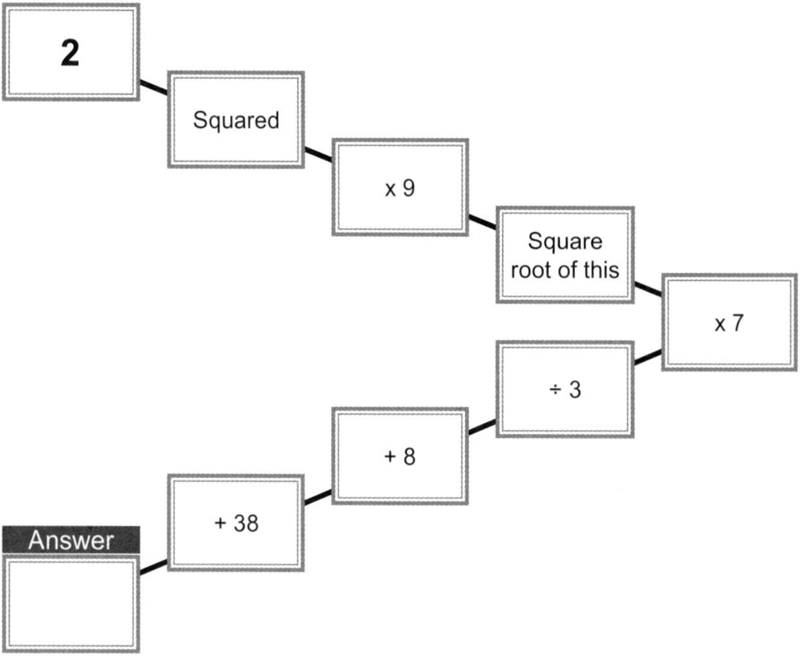

2
Squared
x 9
Square root of this
x 7
÷ 3
+ 8
+ 38
Answer

113

Summing Up

Arrange one of each of the four given numbers, as well as one each of the symbols – (minus), x (times), and + (plus) in every row and column to arrive at the answer at the end of that row or column.

Make the calculations in the order in which they appear: working from left to right, or top to bottom.

2 5
7 9

5	+	7	−	2	x	9	=	90
						−		
							=	12
				7	+		=	54
						x		
							=	78
=		=		=		=		
34		15		16		14		

119

114

Isolate

Draw walls to partition the grid into areas (some walls are already drawn in for you). Each area must contain two circles, area sizes must match those shown by the numbers above the grid and each "+" must be linked to at least two walls.

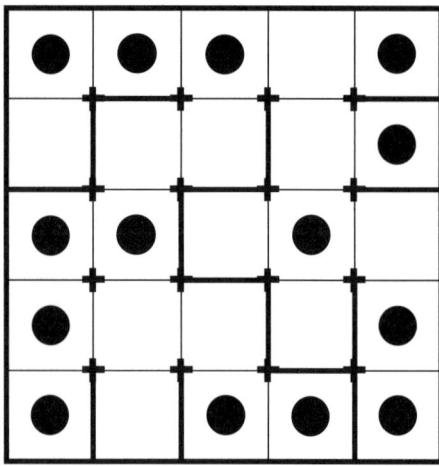

115

Round Up

The number in each circle is the sum of the two numbers below it. Just work out the missing numbers in every circle!

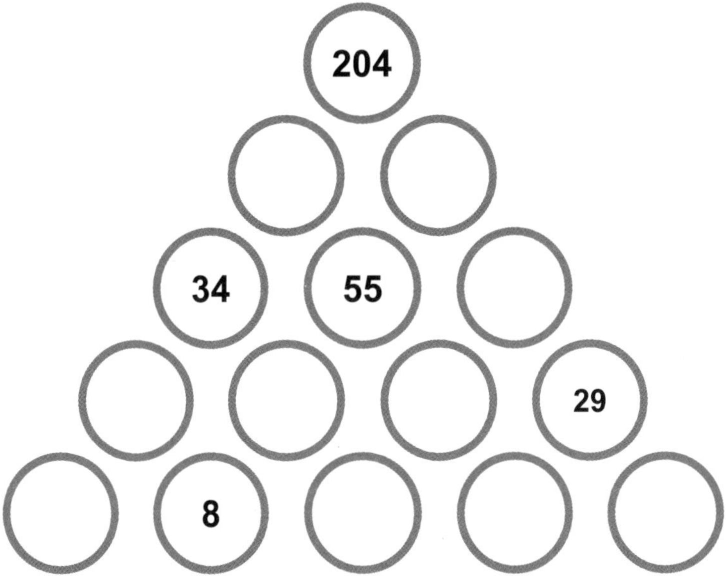

- 204
- 34, 55
- 29
- 8

116

One to Nine

Using the numbers below, complete these six equations (three reading across and three reading down). Every number is used once.

Make the calculations in the order in which they appear: working from left to right, or top to bottom.

1 2 3
4 5 6
7 8 9

	+		−		=	4
+		−		×		
	×		−		=	10
×		+		−		
	−	1	×		=	32
=		=		=		
72		5		36		

117

Number Crunch

Starting at the top left with the number provided, work down from one box to another, applying the mathematical instructions to your running total.

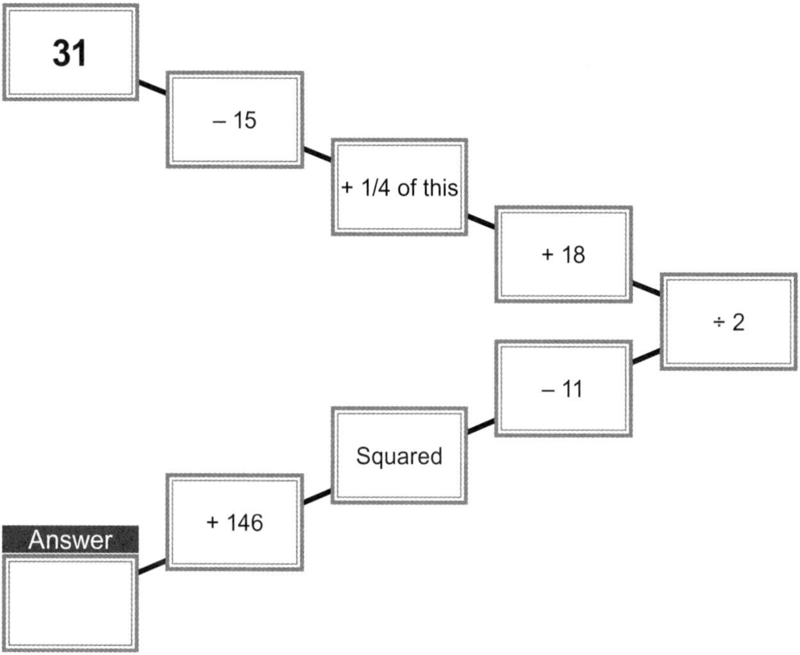

- **31**
- − 15
- + 1/4 of this
- + 18
- ÷ 2
- − 11
- Squared
- + 146
- Answer

118

Summing Up

Arrange one of each of the four given numbers, as well as one each of the symbols – (minus), x (times), and + (plus) in every row and column to arrive at the answer at the end of that row or column.

Make the calculations in the order in which they appear: working from left to right, or top to bottom.

2   5
7   9

5	+	9	x	2	–	7	=	21
							=	12
				9			=	50
					x		=	22
=		=		=		=		
90		15		76		78		

119

Isolate

Draw walls to partition the grid into areas (some walls are already drawn in for you). Each area must contain two circles, area sizes must match those shown by the numbers above the grid and each "+" must be linked to at least two walls.

2 3 3
5 6 6

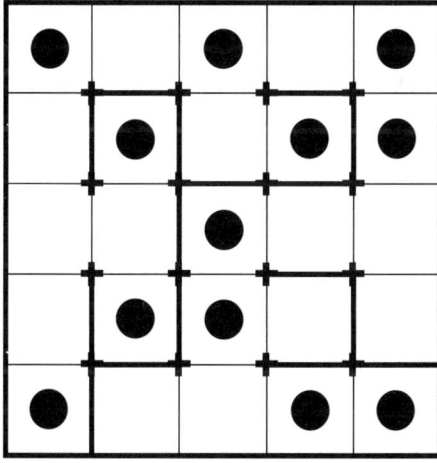

1 MINUTE

120

Round Up

The number in each circle is the sum of the two numbers below it. Just work out the missing numbers in every circle!

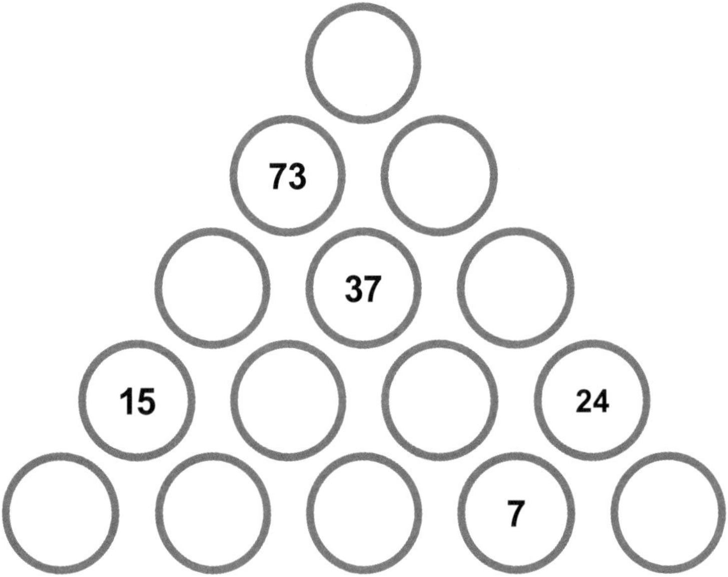

121

One to Nine

Using the numbers below, complete these six equations (three reading across and three reading down). Every number is used once.

Make the calculations in the order in which they appear: working from left to right, or top to bottom.

1 2 3
4 5 6
7 8 9

	−	3	x		=	48
+		x		−		
	+		x		=	40
x		−		x		
	+		−		=	10
=		=		=		
77		14		3		

127

122

Number Crunch

Starting at the top left with the number provided, work down from one box to another, applying the mathematical instructions to your running total.

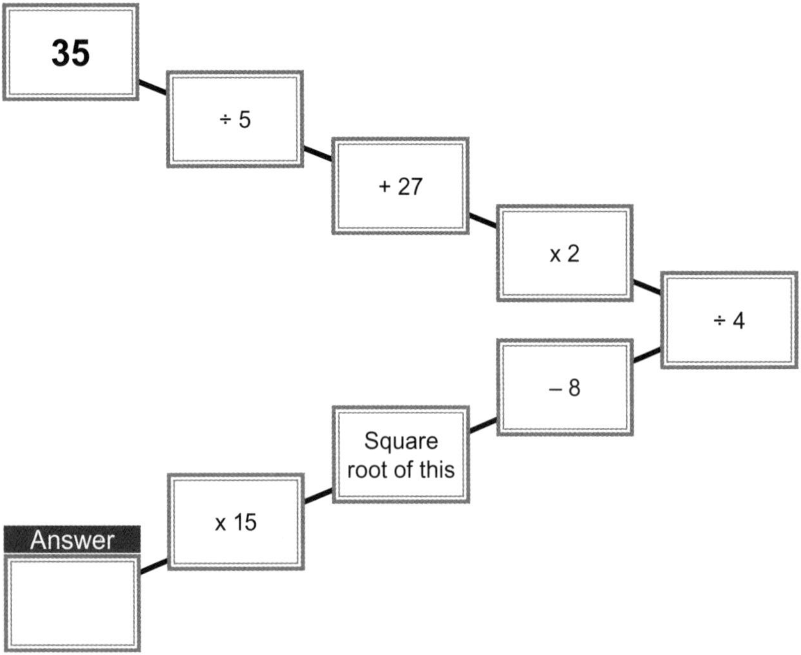

35

÷ 5

+ 27

x 2

÷ 4

− 8

Square root of this

x 15

Answer

123

Summing Up

Arrange one of each of the four given numbers, as well as one each of the symbols – (minus), x (times), and + (plus) in every row and column to arrive at the answer at the end of that row or column.

Make the calculations in the order in which they appear: working from left to right, or top to bottom.

1   3

8   9

9	–	3	+	1	x	8	=	56
				+			=	4
							=	98
						x		
	–						=	90
=		=		=		=		
22		20		78		54		

124

Isolate

Draw walls to partition the grid into areas (some walls are already drawn in for you). Each area must contain two circles, area sizes must match those shown by the numbers above the grid and each "+" must be linked to at least two walls.

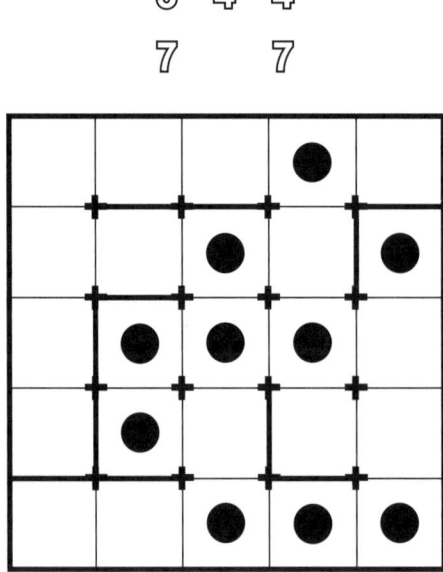

125

Round Up

The number in each circle is the sum of the two numbers below it. Just work out the missing numbers in every circle!

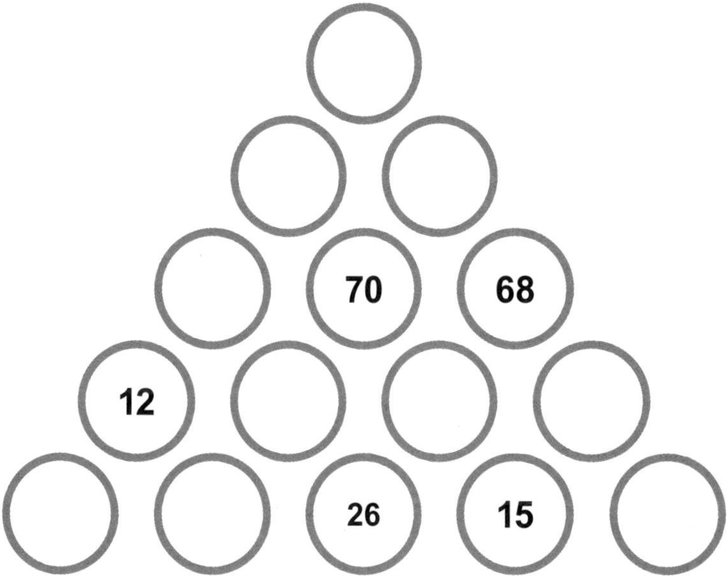

126

One to Nine

Using the numbers below, complete these six equations (three reading across and three reading down). Every number is used once.

Make the calculations in the order in which they appear: working from left to right, or top to bottom.

1 2 3
4 5 6
7 8 9

	+		x		=	35
x		+		−		
	+		−		=	12
−		x		+		
3	x		+		=	24
=		=		=		
21		45		14		

127

Number Crunch

Starting at the top left with the number provided, work down from one box to another, applying the mathematical instructions to your running total.

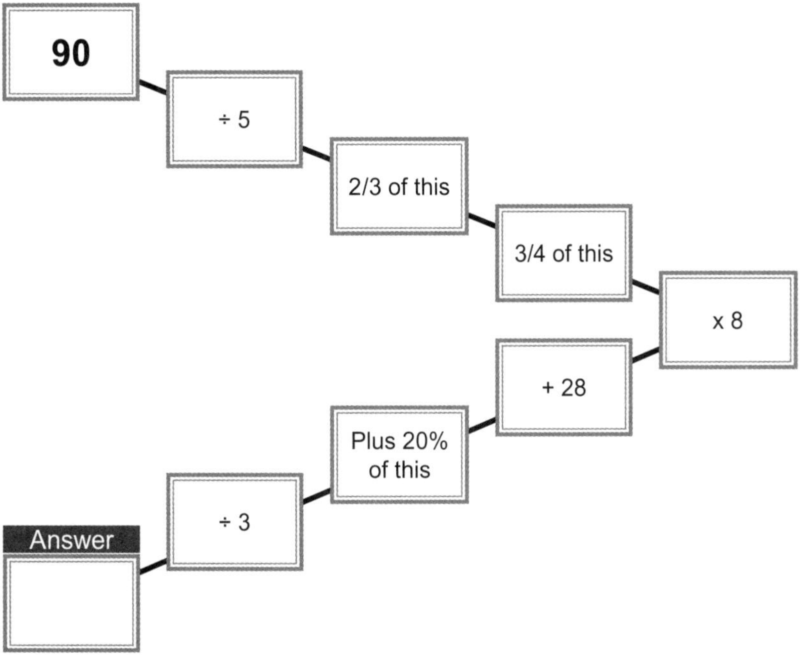

90 → ÷ 5 → 2/3 of this → 3/4 of this → x 8 → + 28 → Plus 20% of this → ÷ 3 → Answer

128

Summing Up

Arrange one of each of the four given numbers, as well as one each of the symbols – (minus), x (times), and + (plus) in every row and column to arrive at the answer at the end of that row or column.

Make the calculations in the order in which they appear: working from left to right, or top to bottom.

2 4
5 8

2	+	8	x	5	–	4	=	46
							=	26
4							=	43
		x						
							=	42
=		=		=		=		
14		30		28		58		

134

129

Isolate

Draw walls to partition the grid into areas (some walls are already drawn in for you). Each area must contain two circles, area sizes must match those shown by the numbers above the grid and each "+" must be linked to at least two walls.

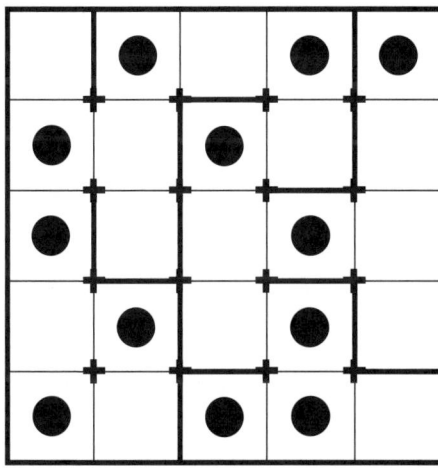

130

Round Up

The number in each circle is the sum of the two numbers below it. Just work out the missing numbers in every circle!

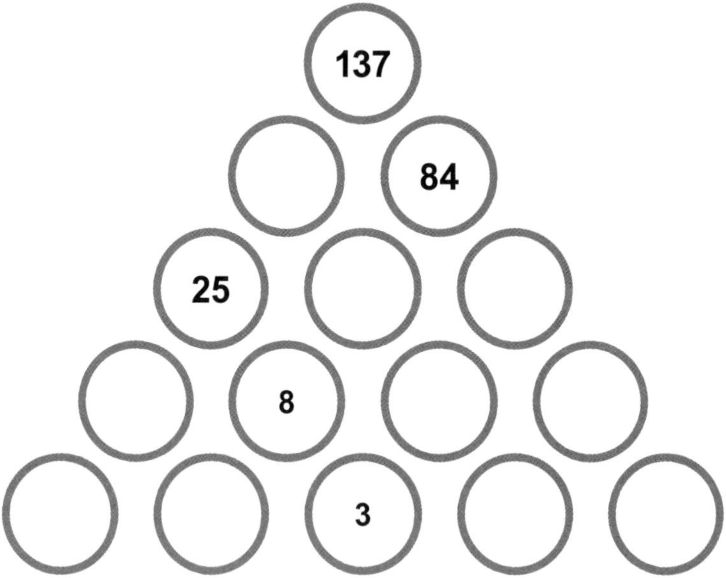

- 137
- 84
- 25
- 8
- 3

131

One to Nine

Using the numbers below, complete these six equations (three reading across and three reading down). Every number is used once.

Make the calculations in the order in which they appear: working from left to right, or top to bottom.

1 2 3
4 5 6
7 8 9

	x		+		=	30
−		+		x		
5	+		x		=	49
+		x		−		
	+		x		=	40
=		=		=		
4		45		38		

132

Number Crunch

Starting at the top left with the number provided, work down from one box to another, applying the mathematical instructions to your running total.

56 → + 15 → − 7 → ÷ 4 → Square root of this → + 69 → − 14 → + 23 → Answer

Pathfinder

The object of this puzzle is to trace a single path from the top left corner to the bottom right corner of the grid, travelling through all of the cells in either a horizontal, vertical, or diagonal direction.

Every cell must be entered once only and your path should take you through the numbers in the sequence 1-2-3-4-5-6-1-2-3-4-5-6, etc.

Can you find the way?

1	3	2	3	6	5
4	2	4	1	4	1
3	5	6	5	2	2
2	1	6	3	1	3
2	4	5	6	4	4
3	1	6	5	5	6

134

Cracker

Given that the letters are valued 1-26 according to their places in the alphabet, can you crack the mystery code to reveal the missing letter?

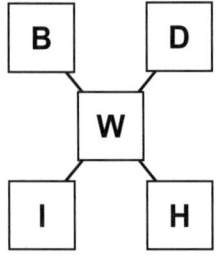
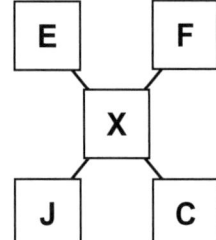
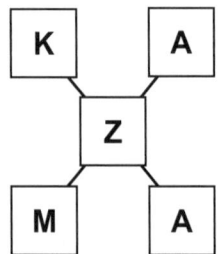
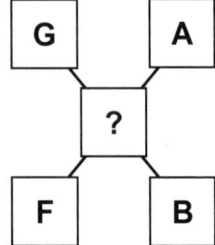

135

What's the Number?

In the diagram below, what number should replace the question mark?

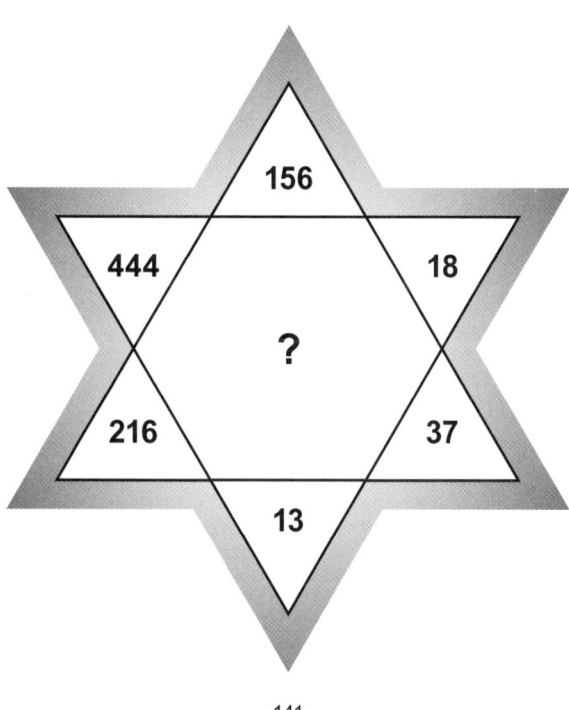

136

One to Nine

Using the numbers below, complete these six equations (three reading across and three reading down). Every number is used once.

Make the calculations in the order in which they appear: working from left to right, or top to bottom.

1 2 3
4 5 6
7 8 9

	−		+		=	12
−		+		x		
	+	7	x		=	50
+		x		−		
	x		+		=	20
=		=		=		
8		48		12		

137

Tile Twister

Place the eight tiles into the puzzle grid so that all adjacent numbers on each tile match up. Tiles may be rotated through 360 degrees, but none may be flipped over.

143

138

Number Crunch

Starting at the top left with the number provided, work down from one box to another, applying the mathematical instructions to your running total.

- **55**
- 4/11 of this
- x 1.75
- 2/7 of this
- x 400%
- + 47
- 2/3 of this
- ÷ 0.5
- Answer

139

Sum Circle

Fill the three empty circles with the symbols +, −, and x in some order, to make a sum that totals the central number. Each symbol must be used once and calculations are made in the direction of travel (clockwise).

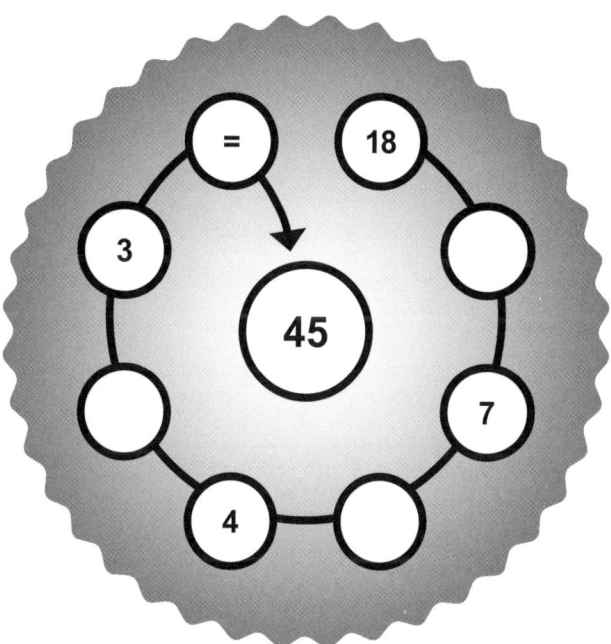

140

Whatever Next?

Which of the four lettered alternatives (A, B, C, or D) fits most logically into the empty square?

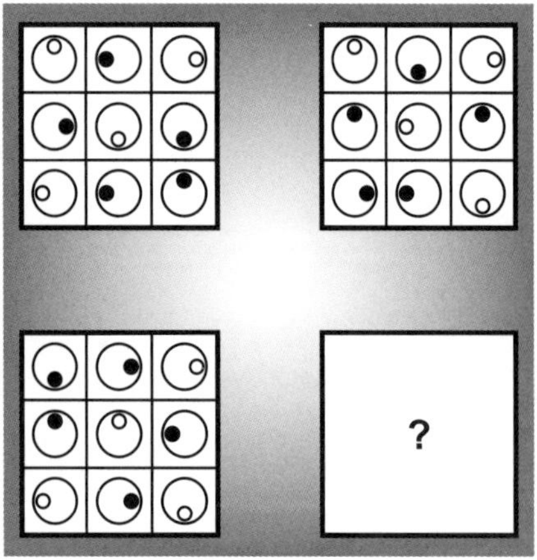

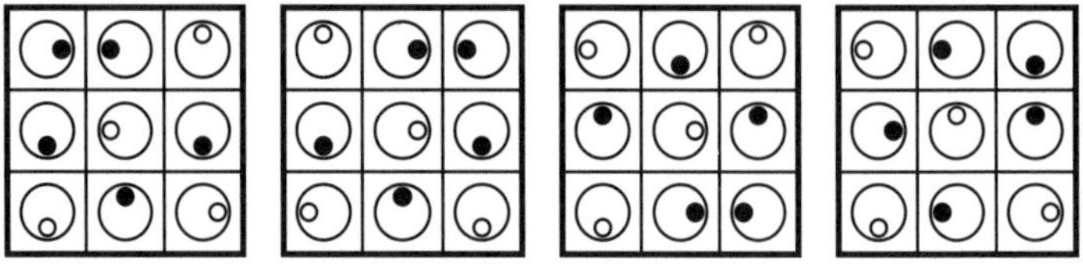

A   B   C   D

141

Clock Work

Draw in the missing hands on the final clock.

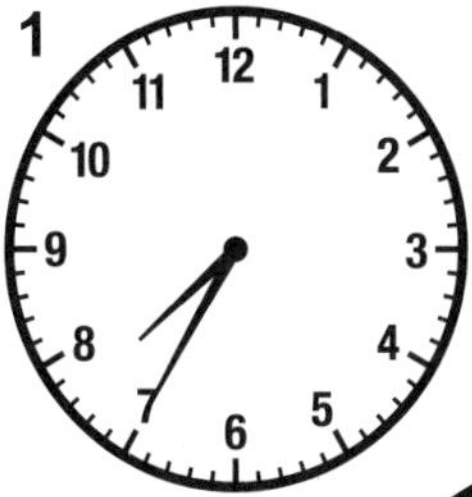

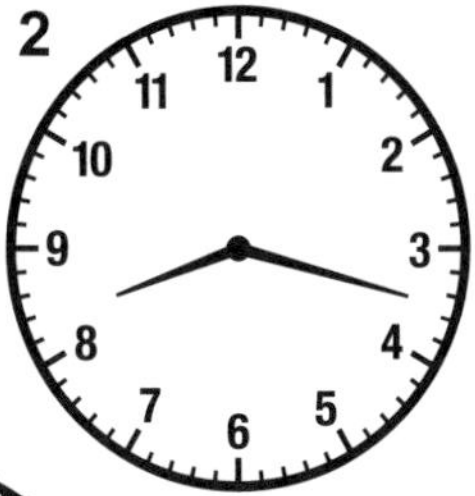

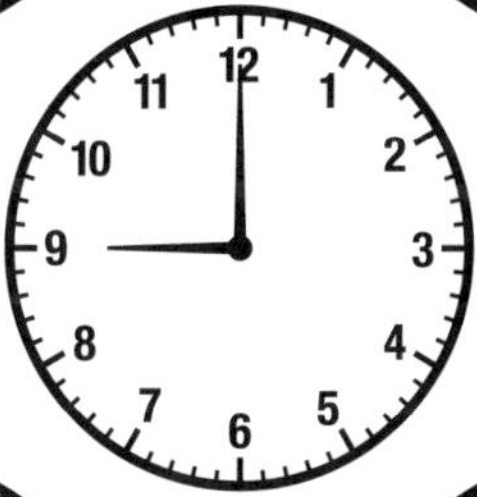

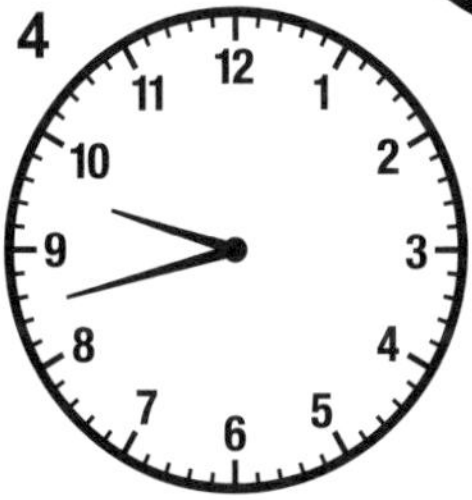

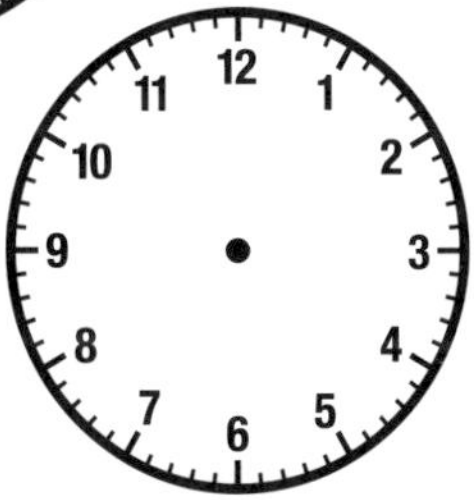

Total Concentration

The blank squares below should be filled with whole numbers between 1 and 30 inclusive, any of which may occur more than once, or not at all.

The numbers in every horizontal row add up to the totals on the right, as do the two long diagonal lines; and those in every vertical column add up to the totals along the bottom.

							119

22		1	18	23	6		121
24			27	16	24	15	138
	17	22	11	3	20		110
23	4	29			9	22	132
25	1		2	29		26	127
8	26	14	18	25		27	128
	13	19		5	19	21	100
121	103	121	104	129	116	162	133

143

Isolate

Draw walls to partition the grid into areas (some walls are already drawn in for you). Each area must contain two circles, area sizes must match those shown by the numbers below and each "+" must be linked to at least two walls.

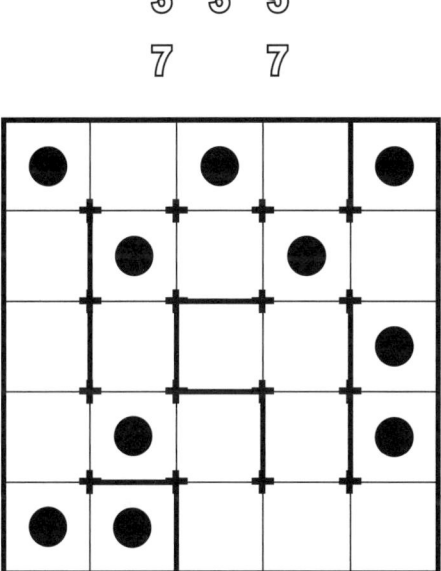

144

Symbol Sums

Each symbol represents a different whole number.

In order to reach the correct total at the end of each row and column, what is the value of the circle, cross, pentagon, square, and star?

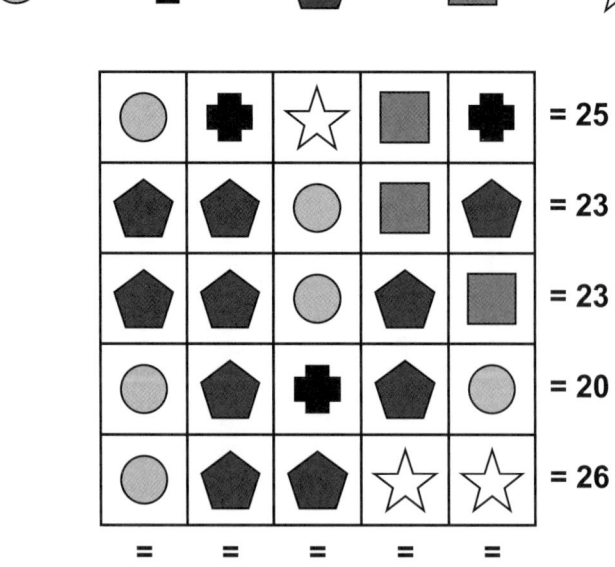

145

Number Link

Working from one square to another, horizontally or vertically (never diagonally), draw single continuous paths to pair up each set of two matching numbers.

No line may cross another and none may travel through any square containing a number.

8				8	9	10	3	4
7				7				
				6			3	
							4	
							2	2
6								11
		11						9
	10				1			1
				5				5

146

Round Up

The number in each circle is the sum of the two numbers below it. Just work out the missing numbers in every circle!

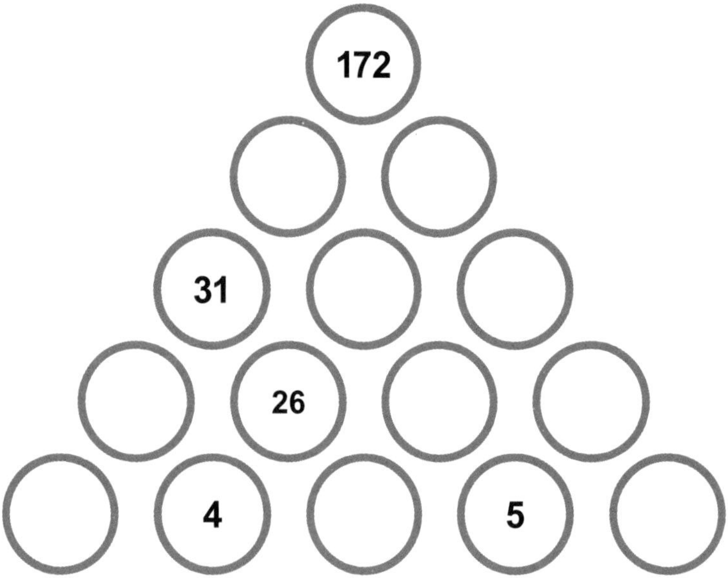

147

Summing Up

Arrange one of each of the four given numbers, as well as one each of the symbols – (minus), x (times), and + (plus) in every row and column to arrive at the answer at the end of that row or column.

Make the calculations in the order in which they appear: working from left to right, or top to bottom.

Numbers: 3, 4, 6, 9

4	+	3	x	9	–	6	=	57
6	–						=	45
							=	15
							=	25
=		=		=		=		
18		33		60		41		

153

148

Numberfit

With the starter already given, can you fit all of the remaining listed numbers into this grid?

2 digits	**3 digits**	**4 digits**			**7 digits**
22	278	1040	3432	4584	5093280
55	885	1084	3780	4880	6223873
	962	1544 ✓	4077	4892	7841903
		2386	4311	5223	9456225
		2847	4511	7891	
		3174	4556	8904	

149

Pathfinder

The object of this puzzle is to trace a single path from the top left corner to the bottom right corner of the grid, travelling through all of the cells in either a horizontal, vertical, or diagonal direction.

Every cell must be entered once only and your path should take you through the numbers in the sequence 1-2-3-4-5-6-1-2-3-4-5-6, etc.

Can you find the way?

1	3	2	1	1	6
2	3	4	6	5	2
6	4	3	5	3	4
5	1	2	4	3	4
5	6	2	2	5	5
4	3	1	1	6	6

150

Cracker

Given that the letters are valued 1-26 according to their places in the alphabet, can you crack the mystery code to reveal the missing letter?

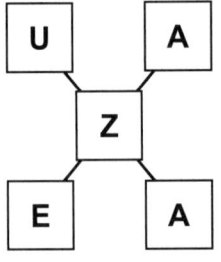
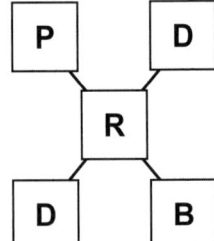
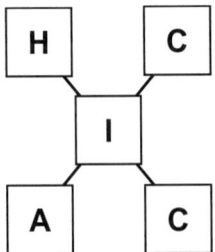
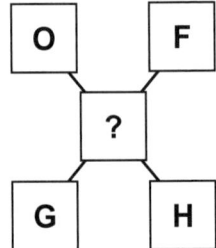

151

What's the Number?

In the diagram below, what number should replace the question mark?

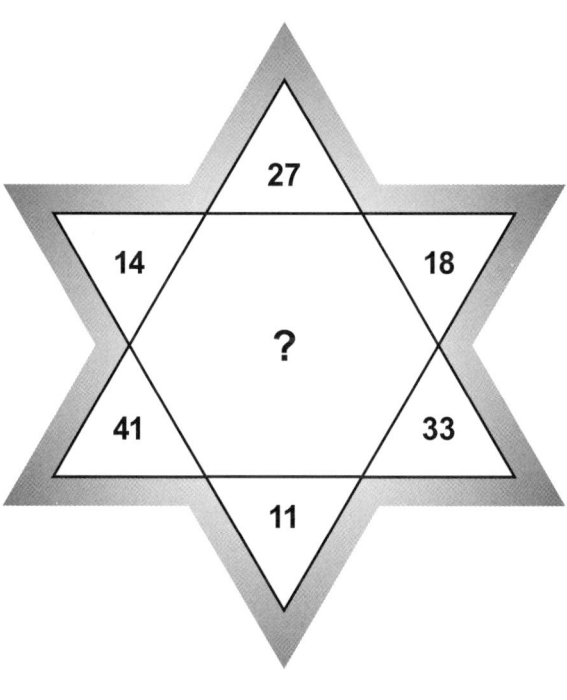

152

One to Nine

Using the numbers below, complete these six equations (three reading across and three reading down). Every number is used once.

Make the calculations in the order in which they appear: working from left to right, or top to bottom.

1 2 3
4 5 6
7 8 9

	x		−		=	5
+		x		+		
	x	6	+		=	15
x		+		−		
	−		x		=	6
=		=		=		
40		23		14		

153

Tile Twister

Place the eight tiles into the puzzle grid so that all adjacent numbers on each tile match up. Tiles may be rotated through 360 degrees, but none may be flipped over.

3	3
4	2

2	1
2	4

2	3
2	1

4	1
4	3

2	4
4	1

2	1
4	2

3	4
2	3

4	2
4	1

154

Number Crunch

Starting at the top left with the number provided, work down from one box to another, applying the mathematical instructions to your running total.

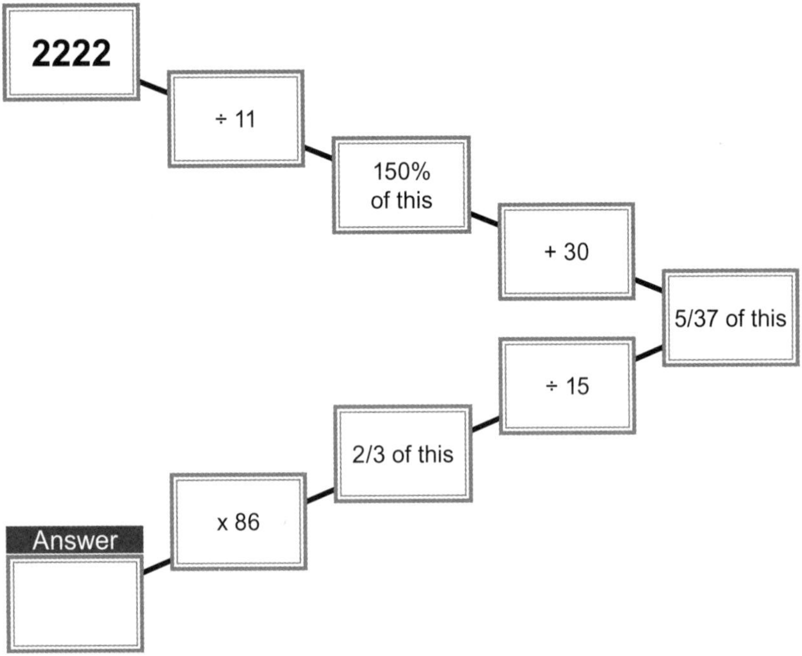

2222

÷ 11

150% of this

+ 30

5/37 of this

÷ 15

2/3 of this

x 86

Answer

155

Sum Circle

Fill the three empty circles with the symbols +, –, and x in some order, to make a sum that totals the central number. Each symbol must be used once and calculations are made in the direction of travel (clockwise).

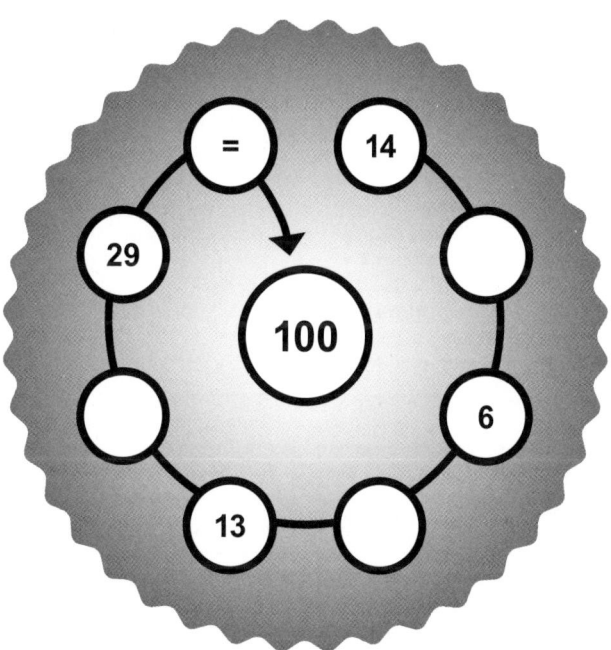

156

Whatever Next?

Which of the four lettered alternatives (A, B, C, or D) fits most logically into the empty square?

D

157

Clock Work

Draw in the missing hands on the final clock.

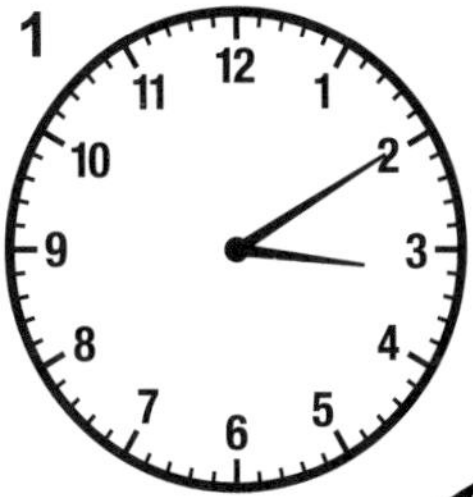

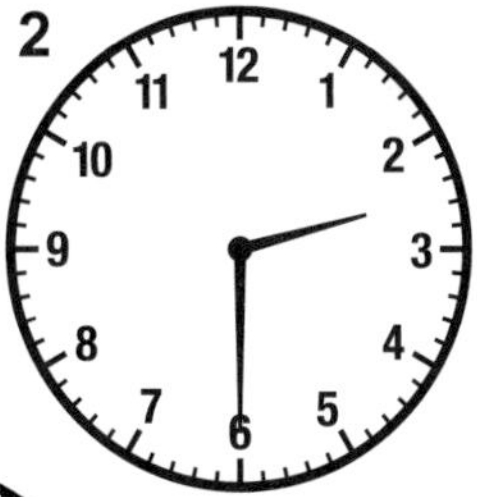

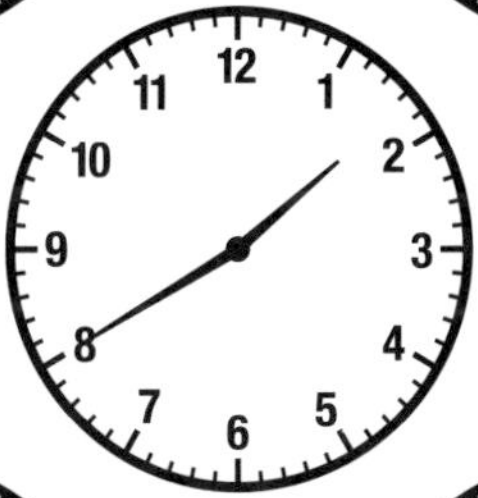

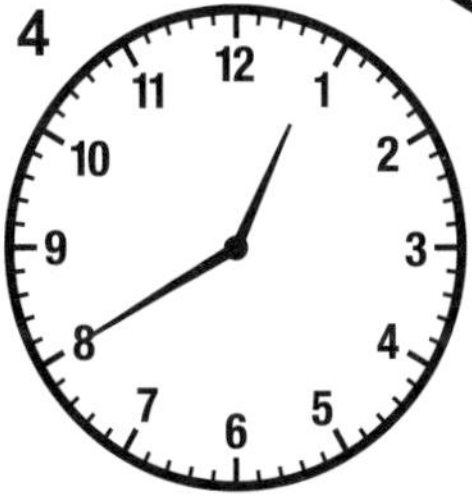

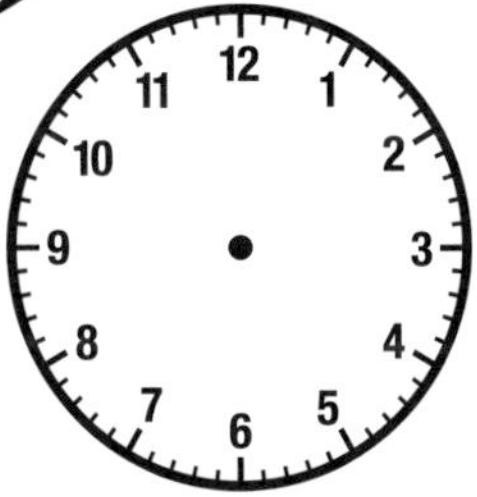

158

Total Concentration

The blank squares below should be filled with whole numbers between 1 and 30 inclusive, any of which may occur more than once, or not at all.

The numbers in every horizontal row add up to the totals on the right, as do the two long diagonal lines; and those in every vertical column add up to the totals along the bottom.

							103
15		7	20	6		18	97
		27	30	22	29	29	164
2	12		4	26	3		96
4	8	24			23	14	111
	21		30	1	17	11	103
22	5		28	19	3		115
10	12	24	9	19		24	127
99	76	135	134	118	119	132	81

159

Isolate

Draw walls to partition the grid into areas (some walls are already drawn in for you). Each area must contain two circles, area sizes must match those shown by the numbers below and each "+" must be linked to at least two walls.

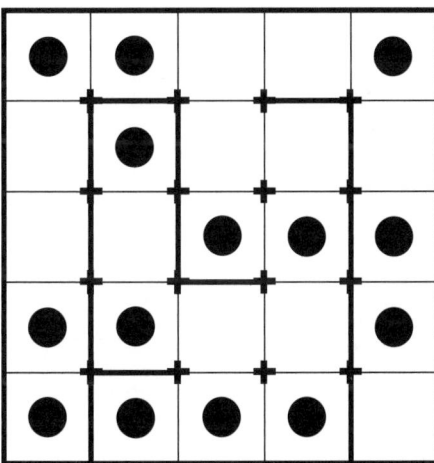

160

Symbol Sums

Each symbol represents a different whole number.

In order to reach the correct total at the end of each row and column, what is the value of the circle, cross, pentagon, square, and star?

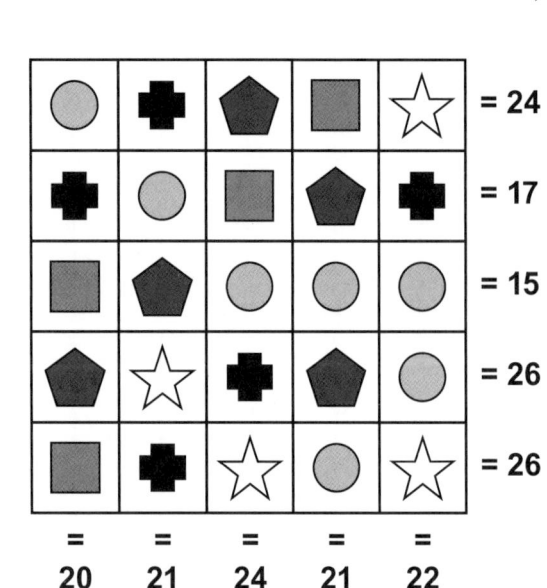

161

Number Link

Working from one square to another, horizontally or vertically (never diagonally), draw single continuous paths to pair up each set of two matching numbers.

No line may cross another and none may travel through any square containing a number.

			10	8	7	3	2	11
	6	5	1					
10							2	
6								
5			1					9
8					7	3	11	
9	4							4

162

Round Up

The number in each circle is the sum of the two numbers below it. Just work out the missing numbers in every circle!

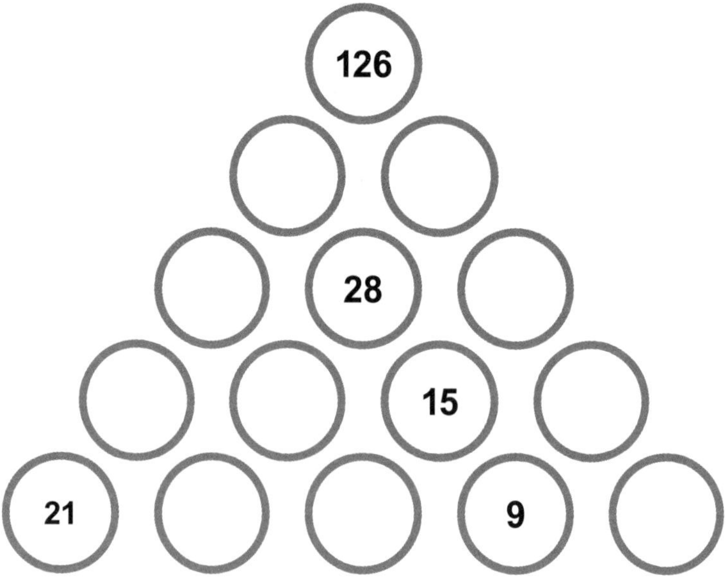

- 126
- 28
- 15
- 21
- 9

163

Summing Up

Arrange one of each of the four given numbers, as well as one each of the symbols – (minus), x (times), and + (plus) in every row and column to arrive at the answer at the end of that row or column.

Make the calculations in the order in which they appear: working from left to right, or top to bottom.

3   4

7   9

9	–	3	+	4	x	7	=	70
x						–		
							=	96
					x			
							=	64
							=	40
=		=		=		=		
32		86		70		25		

164

Numberfit

With the starter already given, can you fit all of the remaining listed numbers into this grid?

3 digits	4 digits			5 digits	
101	1650	5020	8126	14309	67280
330	2672	5318	8719	30392	78475
494	2948	5893	9450	36940	
600	3778	6745	9831	43128	
800	4159	7583		60365	
872 ✓	4668	7862		62271	

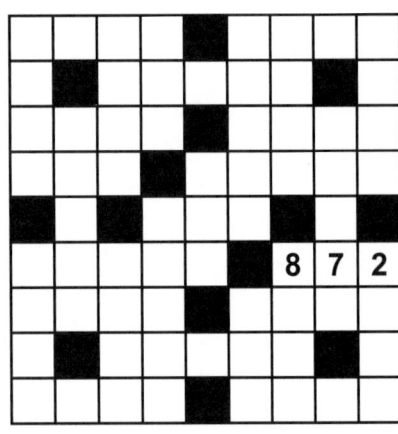

165

Pathfinder

The object of this puzzle is to trace a single path from the top left corner to the bottom right corner of the grid, travelling through all of the cells in either a horizontal, vertical, or diagonal direction.

Every cell must be entered once only and your path should take you through the numbers in the sequence 1-2-3-4-5-6-1-2-3-4-5-6, etc.

Can you find the way?

1	6	5	4	1	2
1	2	3	4	3	6
2	4	6	1	5	3
6	3	5	5	2	4
1	5	4	6	1	5
2	3	4	3	2	6

166

Cracker

Given that the letters are valued 1-26 according to their places in the alphabet, can you crack the mystery code to reveal the missing letter?

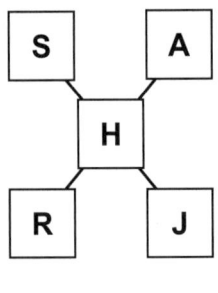
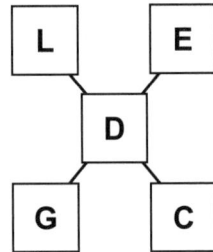
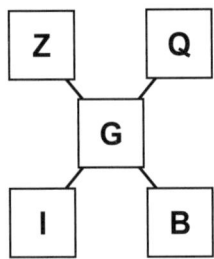
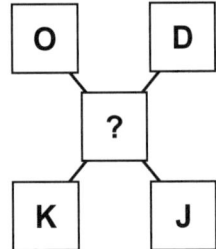

167

Domino Placement

A standard set of 28 dominoes has been laid out as shown. Can you draw in the edges of them all?

The check-box is provided as an aid and the domino already placed will help.

0-0	0-1	0-2	0-3	0-4	0-5	0-6	1-1	1-2	1-3	1-4	1-5	1-6	2-2
			✔										

2-3	2-4	2-5	2-6	3-3	3-4	3-5	3-6	4-4	4-5	4-6	5-5	5-6	6-6

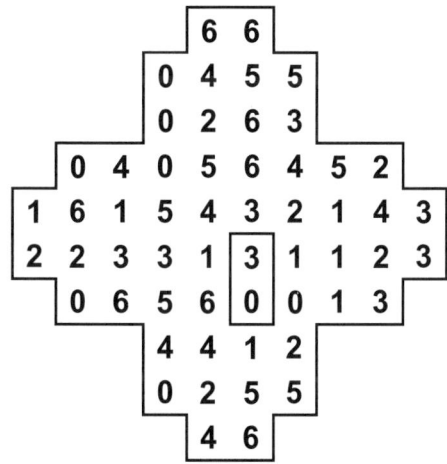

168

More or Less

Fill the grid so that every horizontal row and vertical column contains the numbers 1-5.

The "more than" or "less than" signs are additional clues, indicating where a number is larger or smaller than that in the touching square; in other words, the arrow points towards a number that is lower.

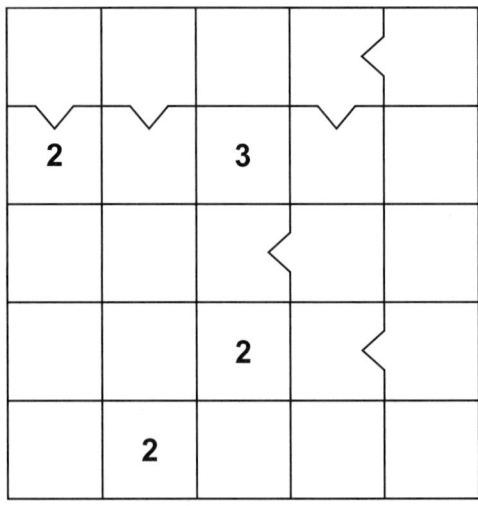

169

One to Nine

Using the numbers below, complete these six equations (three reading across and three reading down). Every number is used once.

Make the calculations in the order in which they appear: working from left to right, or top to bottom.

1 2 3
4 5 6
7 8 9

	+		x		=	22
−		+		x		
	x		+		=	14
x		−		+		
	+		−	3	=	11
=		=		=		
15		4		19		

170

The Bottom Line

Can you fill each square in the bottom line with the correct digit? Every square in the solution contains only one digit from each of the lines above, although two or more squares in the solution may contain the same digit. At the end of every row is a score, which shows:

- **a** the number of digits placed in the correct finishing position on the bottom line, as indicated by a tick; and
- **b** the number of digits which appear on the bottom line, but in a different position, as indicated by a cross.

SCORE

1	1	2	3	✓
2	4	1	5	✓
3	5	5	1	✗
3	6	7	8	✗ ✗
8	2	4	7	✗ ✓
				✓✓✓✓

171

Treasure Hunt

The chart gives directions to a hidden treasure behind the central black square in the grid.

Move the indicated number of spaces north, south, east, and west (eg 4N means move four squares north) stopping at every square once only to arrive there.

At which square should you start?

N

1S	1S	2S	1E	2W
2S	1E	1E	1N	1S
2N	2N	■	1S	1W
1E	1N	1S	1W	2N
2N	2E	2W	1E	1N

W ⇦ (left of row 3) ⇨ **E**

S

3 MINUTES

172

Round Up

The number in each circle is the sum of the two numbers below it. Just work out the missing numbers in every circle!

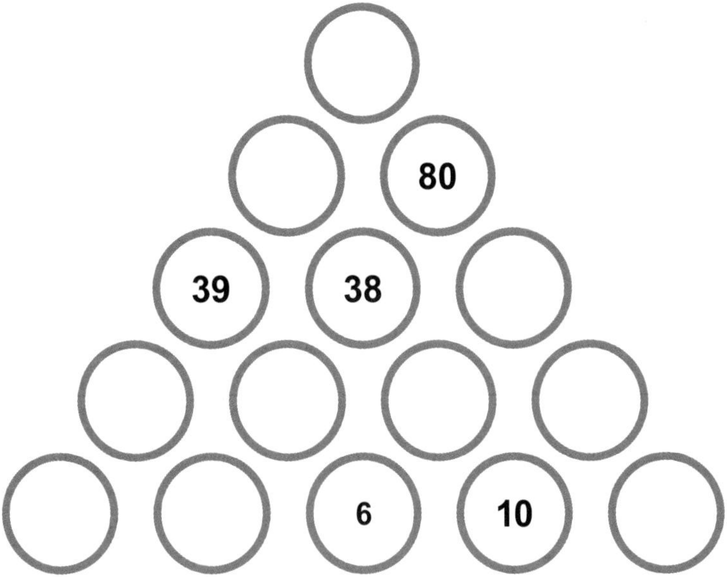

173

Logi-6

Every row and column of this grid should contain one each of the letters A, B, C, D, E, and F.

Each of the six shapes (marked by thicker lines) should also contain one each of the letters A, B, C, D, E, and F.

Can you complete the grid?

D			C	B	A
		C			
E					
					F
	D				

174

Hexagony

Can you place the hexagons into the grid, so that where any hexagon touches another along a straight line, the number in both triangles is the same? No rotation of any hexagon is allowed!

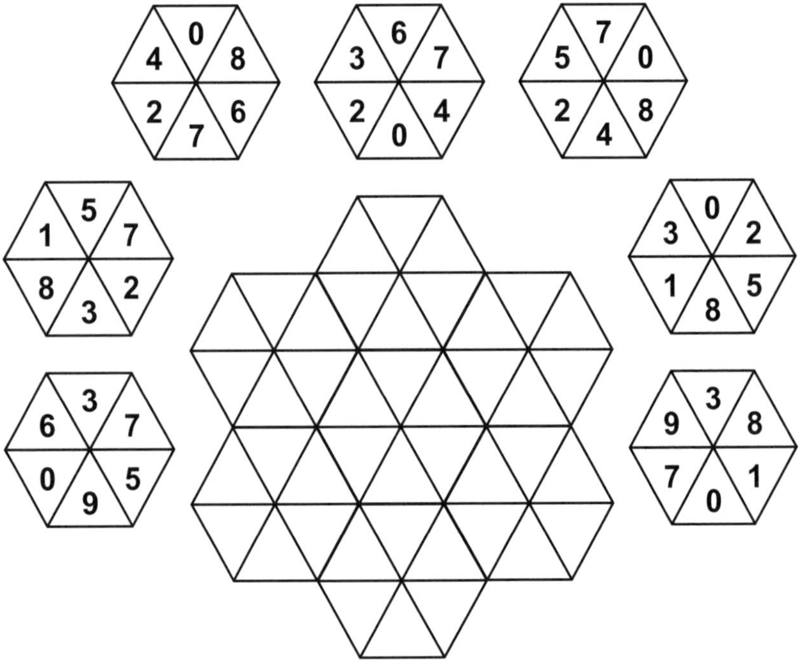

175

Combiku

Each horizontal row and vertical column should contain different shapes and different numbers.

Every square will contain one number and one shape, and no combination may be repeated anywhere else in the puzzle.

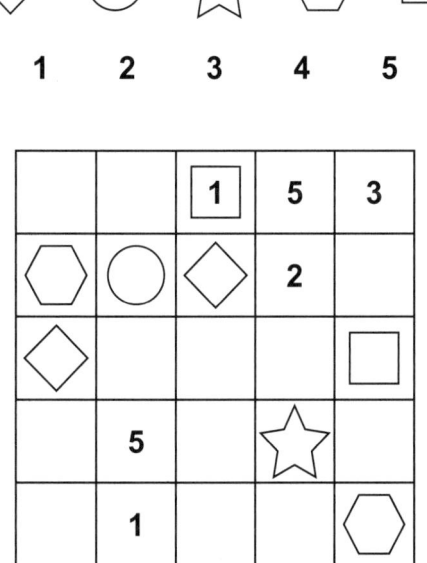

176

Isolate

Draw walls to partition the grid into areas (some walls are already drawn in for you). Each area must contain two circles, area sizes must match those shown by the numbers above the grid and each "+" must be linked to at least two walls.

2 3 4
4 6 6

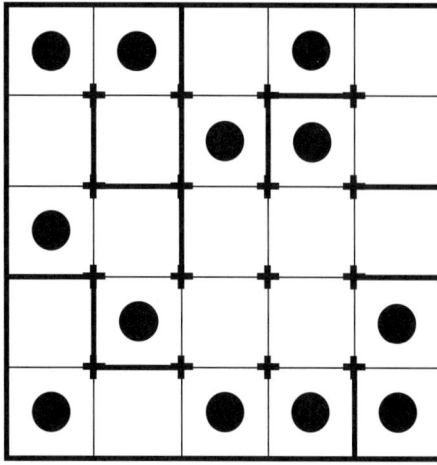

177

It Don't Add Up!

In the square below, change the positions of six numbers, one per horizontal row, vertical column, and long diagonal line of six smaller squares, in such a way that the numbers in each row, column, and long diagonal line total exactly 136.

Any number may appear more than once in a row, column, or line.

34	23	12	19	40	22
27	22	28	11	16	22
24	32	22	28	7	31
21	38	26	9	15	20
26	22	17	36	18	25
12	13	18	26	30	24

3 MINUTES

178

Number Crunch

Starting at the top left with the number provided, work down from one box to another, applying the mathematical instructions to your running total.

247

3/13 of this

5/19 of this

x 35

5/21 of this

Cube root of this

x 1.4

x 45

Answer

179

Summing Up

Arrange one of each of the four given numbers, as well as one each of the symbols – (minus), x (times), and + (plus) in every row and column to arrive at the answer at the end of that row or column.

Make the calculations in the order in which they appear: working from left to right, or top to bottom.

4   6
7   9

9	–	4	x	7	+	6	=	41
						x		
							=	53
–								
							=	31
	–				x		=	40
=		=		=		=		
77		35		81		37		

180

Eliminator

Every oval shape in this diagram should contain a different letter of the alphabet from A to K inclusive.

Use the clues to determine their locations. Reference in the clues to "due" means in any location along the same horizontal or vertical line.

1 The A is due south of the F and due east of the B.

2 The B is due north of the E and due west of the I.

3 The C is due north of the I and due east of the J.

4 The D is due north of the K.

5 The E is due south of the H and due west of the G.

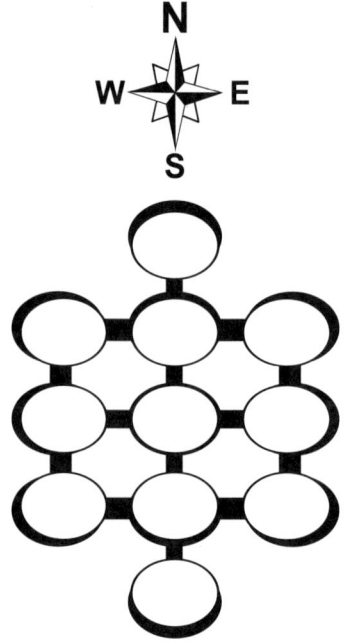

181

Where the L?

Twelve L-shapes like the ones here need to be inserted in the grid, and each L has one hole in it.

There are three pieces of each of the four kinds shown here, and any piece may be turned or flipped over before being put in the grid. No pieces of the same kind touch, even at a corner.

The pieces fit together so well that you cannot see any spaces between them; only the holes show. Can you tell where the Ls are?

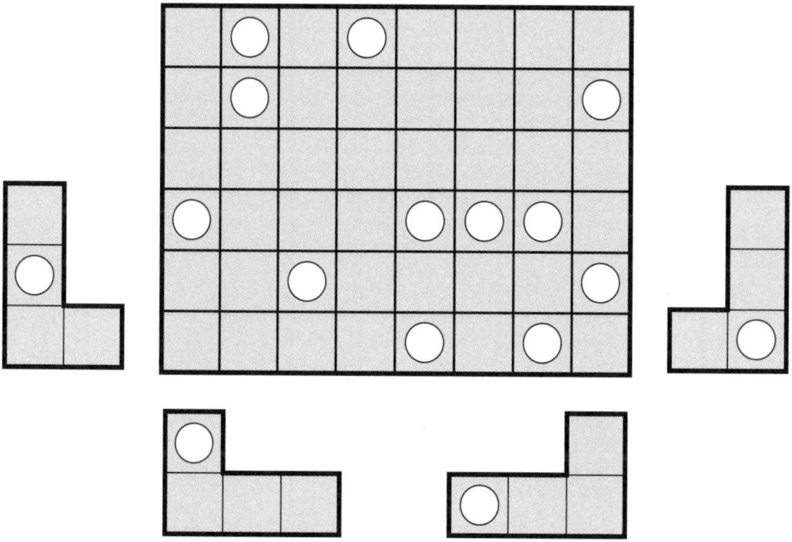

182

Sudoku

Every row, every column, and each of the nine smaller boxes of nine squares should be filled with a different number from 1 to 9 inclusive.

Some numbers are already in place. Can you complete the grid?

		7	2	5				
	6	4	3				2	
5						3	1	9
2			7	3		1		4
		5	1		6	9		
7		6		8	4			3
8	7	9						5
	2				9	6	8	
				4	3	7		

183

Domino Placement

A standard set of 28 dominoes has been laid out as shown. Can you draw in the edges of them all?

The check-box is provided as an aid and the domino already placed will help.

0-0	0-1	0-2	0-3	0-4	0-5	0-6	1-1	1-2	1-3	1-4	1-5	1-6	2-2

2-3	2-4	2-5	2-6	3-3	3-4	3-5	3-6	4-4	4-5	4-6	5-5	5-6	6-6
											✓		

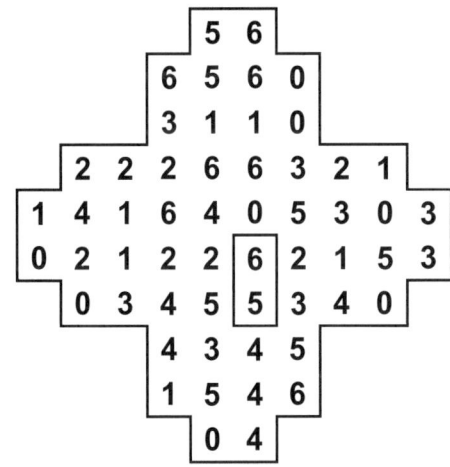

184

More or Less

Fill the grid so that every horizontal row and vertical column contains the numbers 1-5.

The "more than" or "less than" signs are additional clues, indicating where a number is larger or smaller than that in the touching square; in other words, the arrow points towards a number that is lower.

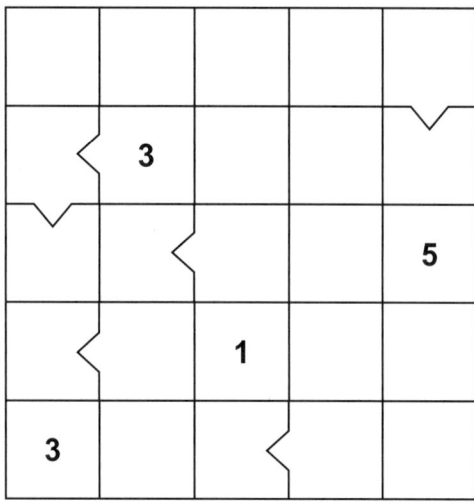

185

One to Nine

Using the numbers below, complete these six equations (three reading across and three reading down). Every number is used once.

Make the calculations in the order in which they appear: working from left to right, or top to bottom.

1 2 3
4 5 6
7 8 9

	−		×		=	35
×		+		−		
	+		×		=	11
−		×		×		
	×		−	6	=	18
=		=		=		
33		72		24		

186

The Bottom Line

Can you fill each square in the bottom line with the correct digit? Every square in the solution contains only one digit from each of the lines above, although two or more squares in the solution may contain the same digit. At the end of every row is a score, which shows:

a   the number of digits placed in the correct finishing position on the bottom line, as indicated by a tick; and

b   the number of digits which appear on the bottom line, but in a different position, as indicated by a cross.

SCORE

1	2	3	4	✓✓
1	4	5	2	✗✗
2	6	7	3	✗✗
3	4	1	8	✗✗
4	1	8	5	✗✗
				✓✓✓✓

187

Treasure Hunt

The chart gives directions to a hidden treasure behind the central black square in the grid.

Move the indicated number of spaces north, south, east, and west (eg 4N means move four squares north) stopping at every square once only to arrive there.

At which square should you start?

N ⇧

1S	2E	2W	1E	2S
1E	2S	1N	2S	1W
1S	2N	■	2S	2W
2E	1N	2N	1N	2N
2N	1E	2W	2W	1N

W ⇦ (left of row 3) ⇨ E

⇩ **S**

188

Round Up

The number in each circle is the sum of the two numbers below it. Just work out the missing numbers in every circle!

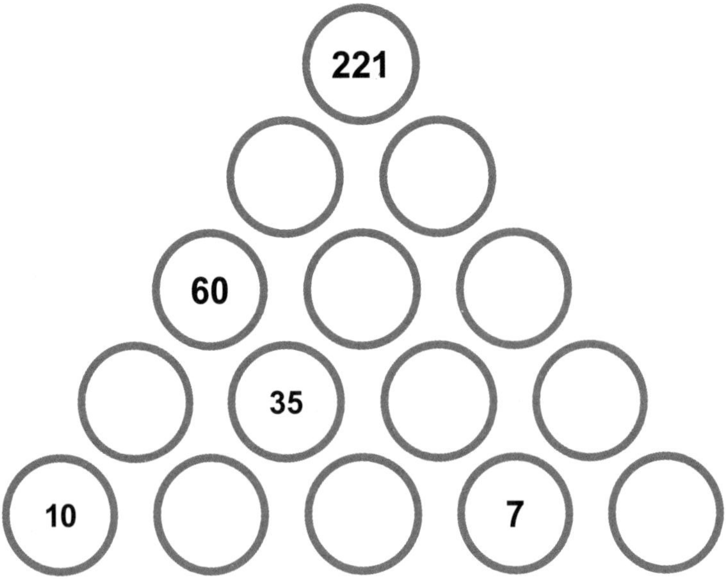

189

Logi-6

Every row and column of this grid should contain one each of the letters A, B, C, D, E, and F.

Each of the six shapes (marked by thicker lines) should also contain one each of the letters A, B, C, D, E, and F.

Can you complete the grid?

	A				
				F	
C					
			A		
		C	B		
F		E			D

3 MINUTES

190

Hexagony

Can you place the hexagons into the grid, so that where any hexagon touches another along a straight line, the number in both triangles is the same? No rotation of any hexagon is allowed!

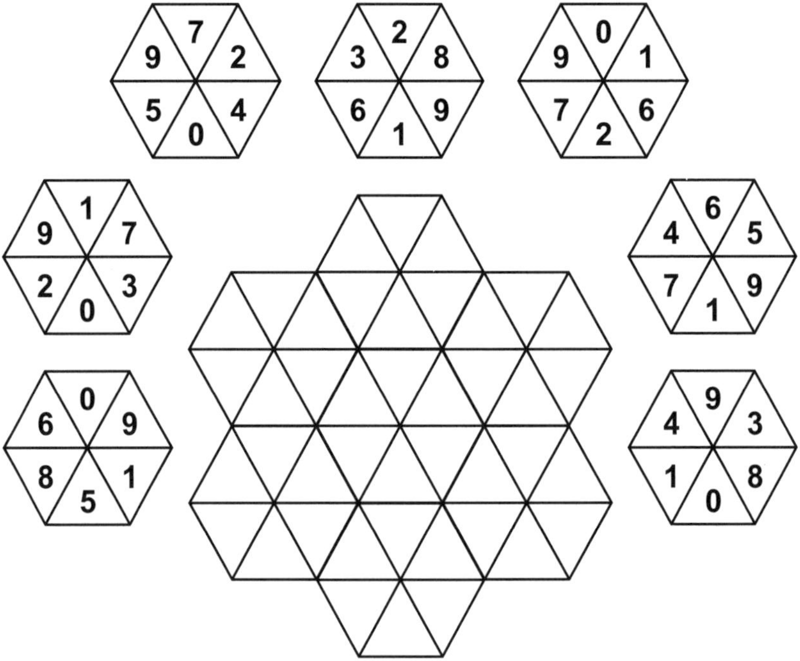

191

Combiku

Each horizontal row and vertical column should contain different shapes and different numbers.

Every square will contain one number and one shape, and no combination may be repeated anywhere else in the puzzle.

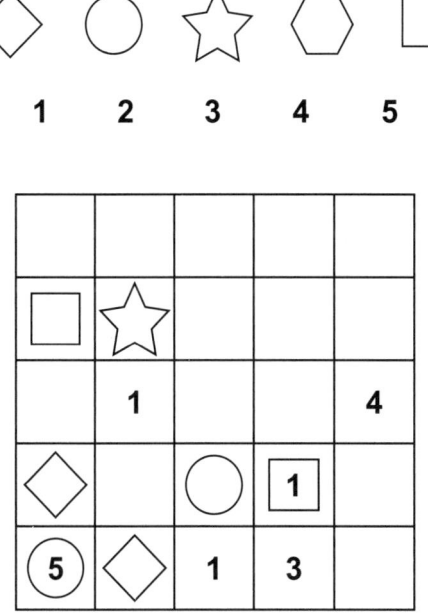

192

Isolate

Draw walls to partition the grid into areas (some walls are already drawn in for you). Each area must contain two circles, area sizes must match those shown by the numbers above the grid and each "+" must be linked to at least two walls.

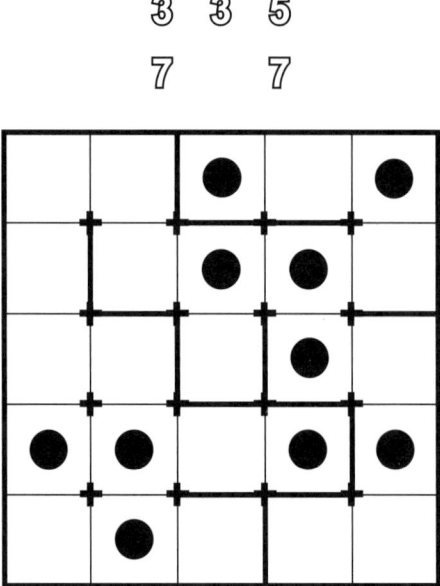

193

It Don't Add Up!

In the square below, change the positions of six numbers, one per horizontal row, vertical column, and long diagonal line of six smaller squares, in such a way that the numbers in each row, column, and long diagonal line total exactly 101.

Any number may appear more than once in a row, column, or line.

16	11	21	18	27	16
22	16	18	9	18	15
15	23	16	20	9	13
28	27	21	12	5	18
13	6	19	20	21	19
17	13	14	19	18	13

3 MINUTES

194

Number Crunch

Starting at the top left with the number provided, work down from one box to another, applying the mathematical instructions to your running total.

33

x 25

2/3 of this

9/11 of this

28% of this

5/14 of this

+ 89

÷ 0.25

Answer

195

Summing Up

Arrange one of each of the four given numbers, as well as one each of the symbols – (minus), x (times), and + (plus) in every row and column to arrive at the answer at the end of that row or column.

Make the calculations in the order in which they appear: working from left to right, or top to bottom.

3 5
7 8

3	+	8	–	7	x	5	=	20
							=	40
		x						
				5			=	42
							=	16
=		=		=		=		
14		8		54		57		

196

Eliminator

Every oval shape in this diagram should contain a different letter of the alphabet from A to K inclusive.

Use the clues to determine their locations. Reference in the clues to "due" means in any location along the same horizontal or vertical line.

1. The A is due south of the D and due east of the I.
2. The B is due north of the E.
3. The C is due east of the E and due north of the G.
4. The F is due south of the D, which is due east of the H.
5. The D is due west of the J and due south of the B.

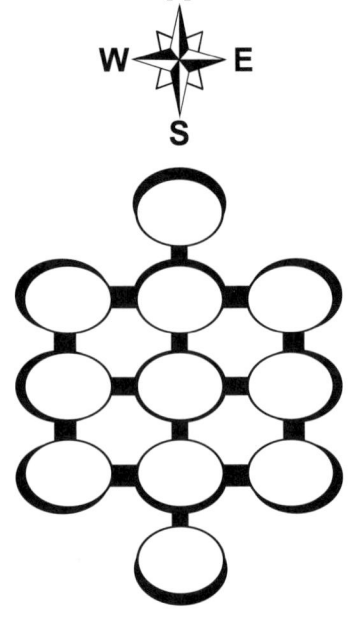

197

Where the L?

Twelve L-shapes like the ones here need to be inserted in the grid, and each L has one hole in it.

There are three pieces of each of the four kinds shown here, and any piece may be turned or flipped over before being put in the grid. No pieces of the same kind touch, even at a corner.

The pieces fit together so well that you cannot see any spaces between them; only the holes show. Can you tell where the Ls are?

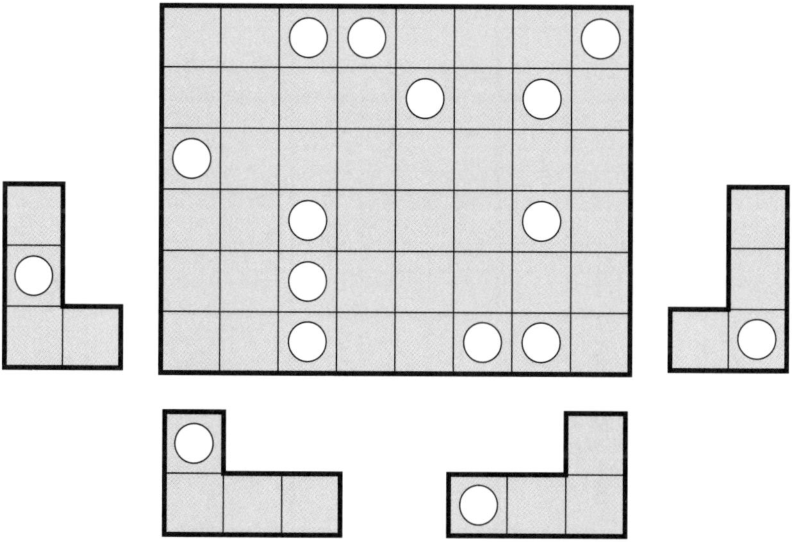

Sudoku

Every row, every column, and each of the nine smaller boxes of nine squares should be filled with a different number from 1 to 9 inclusive.

Some numbers are already in place. Can you complete the grid?

		1			9		7	
5			8	7			1	3
4					5	6	8	
2		7		9			5	
		3	5		8	9		
	4			3		1		8
	5	9	1					2
1	2			6	7			4
	6		2			8		

199

Domino Placement

A standard set of 28 dominoes has been laid out as shown. Can you draw in the edges of them all?

The check-box is provided as an aid and the domino already placed will help.

0-0	0-1	0-2	0-3	0-4	0-5	0-6	1-1	1-2	1-3	1-4	1-5	1-6	2-2
✔													

2-3	2-4	2-5	2-6	3-3	3-4	3-5	3-6	4-4	4-5	4-6	5-5	5-6	6-6

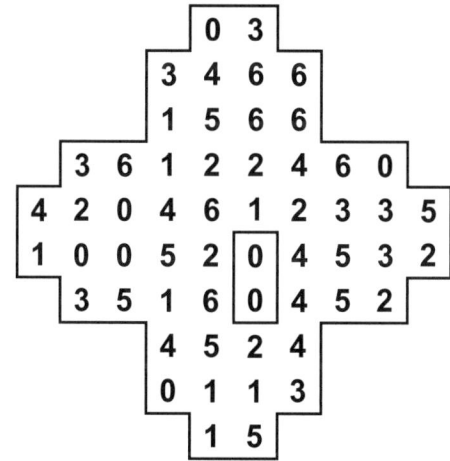

205

200

More or Less

Fill the grid so that every horizontal row and vertical column contains the numbers 1-5.

The "more than" or "less than" signs are additional clues, indicating where a number is larger or smaller than that in the touching square; in other words, the arrow points towards a number that is lower.

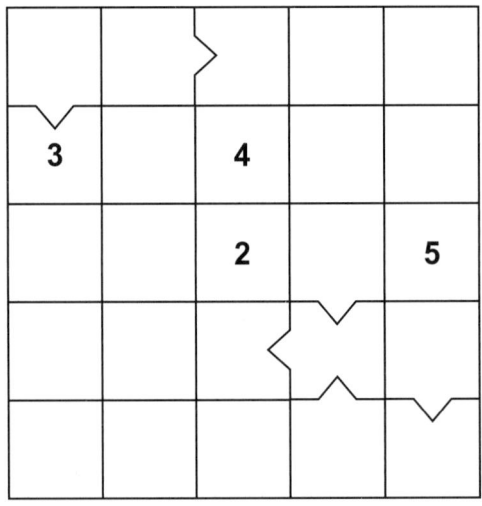

1

5	x	1	+	3	=	8
+		x		+		
9	−	6	x	8	=	24
x		−		x		
2	+	4	x	7	=	42
=		=		=		
28		2		77		

2

$187 - 16 = 171$,
$171 \div 9 = 19$,
$19 - 4 = 15$,
$15^2 = 225$,
$225 \div 25 = 9$,
$9 + 5 = 14$,
$14 + 73 = 87$.

3

7	+	9	−	4	x	8	=	96
x		−		+		−		
8	−	4	x	9	+	7	=	43
+		x		−		+		
4	x	8	−	7	+	9	=	34
−		+		x		x		
9	−	7	x	8	+	4	=	20
=		=		=		=		
51		47		48		40		

4

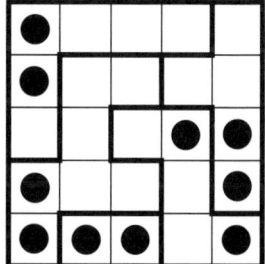

5

```
            231
         100   131
       40   60   71
     19   21   39   32
   6    13    8    31    1
```

6

3	+	7	x	5	=	50
+		+		+		
1	x	4	+	9	=	13
x		x		x		
6	+	8	−	2	=	12
=		=		=		
24		88		28		

7

522 ÷ 9 = 58,
58 + 12 = 70,
10% of 70 = 7,
7 x 5 = 35,
35 + 45 = 80,
80 x 1.05 = 84,
84 ÷ 12 = 7.

8

4	+	7	−	8	x	3	=	9
x		−		−		+		
8	−	3	x	4	+	7	=	27
−		x		+		x		
7	x	8	−	3	+	4	=	57
+		+		x		−		
3	+	4	x	7	−	8	=	41
=		=		=		=		
28		36		49		32		

9

10

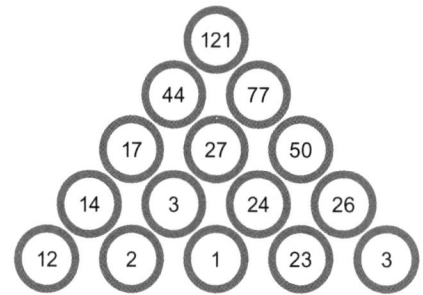

11

6	−	4	x	8	=	16
x		+		−		
1	+	7	x	5	=	40
+		x		+		
9	x	3	−	2	=	25
=		=		=		
15		33		5		

12

Square root of 169 = 13,
13 x 4 = 52,
52 + 15 = 67,
67 − 27 = 40,
15% of 40 = 6,
6 + 17 = 23,
23 x 8 = 184.

13

9	−	1	+	8	x	6	=	96
x		+		−		x		
6	+	8	x	1	−	9	=	5
−		−		x		−		
8	−	6	x	9	+	1	=	19
+		x		+		+		
1	x	9	−	6	+	8	=	11
=		=		=		=		
47		27		69		61		

14

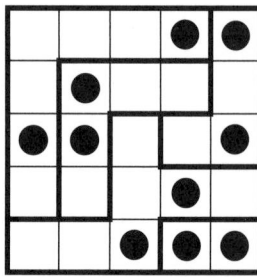

15

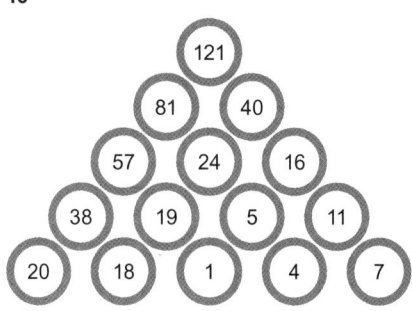

16

3	x	1	+	7	=	10
+		x		−		
6	+	8	x	5	=	70
x		−		x		
4	−	2	+	9	=	11
=		=		=		
36		6		18		

17

$235 \div 5 = 47$,
$47 \times 2 = 94$,
$94 - 19 = 75$,
$75 \times 9 = 675$,
$675 + 215 = 890$,
$890 + 89 = 979$,
$979 - 190 = 789$.

18

7	−	1	+	6	x	8	=	96
x		+		x		−		
8	+	6	x	7	−	1	=	97
−		x		+		x		
6	x	8	−	1	+	7	=	54
+		−		−		+		
1	x	7	+	8	−	6	=	9
=		=		=		=		
51		49		35		55		

19

20

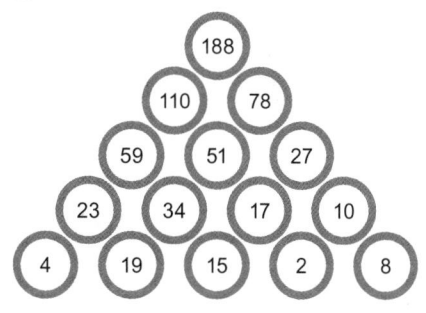

21

5	x	7	−	2	=	33
−		+		x		
4	+	9	−	6	=	7
x		x		+		
8	−	1	x	3	=	21
=		=		=		
8		16		15		

22

$15 \div 3 \times 2 = 10$,
$10 + 20\% = 12$,
$12 \times 14 = 168$,
$168 \div 3 = 56$,
$56 - 27 = 29$,
$29 \times 2 = 58$,
$58 + 142 = 200$.

23

4	+	8	−	2	x	6	=	60
x		−		+		x		
2	x	6	+	4	−	8	=	8
+		+		x		−		
8	−	2	+	6	x	4	=	48
−		x		−		+		
6	+	4	x	8	−	2	=	78
=		=		=		=		
10		16		28		46		

24

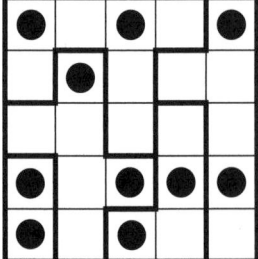

25

```
           189
         84  105
       37  47  58
     12  25  22  36
    2  10  15   7  29
```

26

6	−	1	x	5	=	25
+		+		x		
2	x	4	+	8	=	16
x		x		−		
7	+	9	x	3	=	48
=		=		=		
56		45		37		

27

61 + 5 = 66,
66 ÷ 11 = 6,
6 x 13 = 78,
78 ÷ 3 x 2 = 52,
52 ÷ 2 = 26,
26 − 8 = 18,
18 x 3 = 54.

28

8	−	4	+	7	x	5	=	55
−		x		−		+		
5	+	7	x	4	−	8	=	40
x		−		x		−		
7	x	5	+	8	−	4	=	39
+		+		+		x		
4	+	8	−	5	x	7	=	49
=		=		=		=		
25		31		29		63		

29

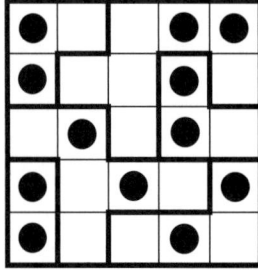

30

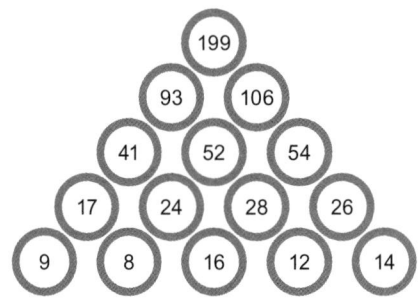

31

1	x	9	+	5	=	14
x		−		+		
4	−	3	x	7	=	7
+		x		x		
6	+	8	−	2	=	12
=		=		=		
10		48		24		

32

$10^2 = 100$,
$100 - 14 = 86$,
$86 \div 2 = 43$,
$43 + 17 = 60$,
20% of $60 = 12$,
$12^2 = 144$,
$144 + 56 = 200$.

33

3	+	5	x	4	−	9	=	23
+		−		x		−		
9	−	4	x	5	+	3	=	28
−		x		−		x		
4	x	9	−	3	+	5	=	38
x		+		+		+		
5	−	3	x	9	+	4	=	22
=		=		=		=		
40		12		26		34		

34

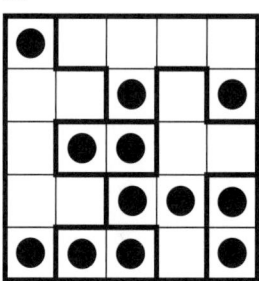

35

```
                183
             67     116
          17    50     66
        3    14    36    30
      1    2    12    24    6
```

36

4	+	8	−	6	=	6
x		−		+		
1	x	5	+	3	=	8
+		x		−		
9	−	7	x	2	=	4
=		=		=		
13		21		7		

37

$6 \times 13 = 78$,
$78 \div 3 = 26$,
$26 + 78 = 104$,
$104 \times 2 = 208$,
$208 \div 4 = 52$,
$52 - 18 = 34$,
$34 \div 2 = 17$.

38

5	x	3	−	9	+	6	=	12
−		+		x		x		
3	x	6	+	5	−	9	=	14
x		−		−		−		
9	−	5	x	6	+	3	=	27
+		x		+		+		
6	+	9	x	3	−	5	=	40
=		=		=		=		
24		36		42		56		

39

40

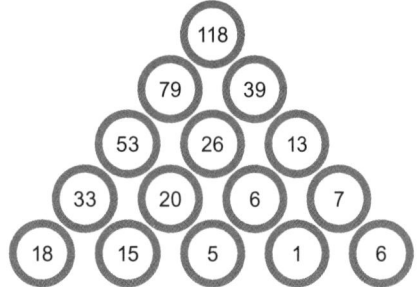

41

5	+	8	−	1	=	12
x		−		+		
3	x	7	+	9	=	30
+		x		x		
6	−	2	x	4	=	16
=		=		=		
21		2		40		

42

$111 \div 3 = 37$,
$37 - 12 = 25$,
Square root of $25 = 5$,
$5 \times 15 = 75$,
$75 + 105 = 180$,
5% of $180 = 9$,
Square root of $9 = 3$.

43

9	−	2	+	4	x	3	=	33
+		x		+		−		
3	+	4	x	9	−	2	=	61
x		+		x		+		
2	x	9	−	3	+	4	=	19
−		−		−		x		
4	−	3	+	2	x	9	=	27
=		=		=		=		
20		14		37		45		

44

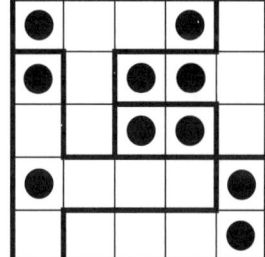

45

```
            (104)
         (50) (54)
       (29) (21) (33)
     (21) (8) (13) (20)
   (20) (1) (7) (6) (14)
```

46

6	+	9	x	2	=	30
−		−		x		
4	x	7	−	5	=	23
x		x		+		
1	x	3	+	8	=	11
=		=		=		
2		6		18		

47

50% of 250 = 125,
125 ÷ 5 = 25,
25 x 7 = 175,
175 x 2 = 350,
350 + 40 = 390,
390 x 1.2 = 468,
468 ÷ 9 = 52.

48

6	+	3	−	8	x	2	=	2
x		+		−		x		
3	x	8	+	2	−	6	=	20
−		x		x		+		
8	−	2	+	6	x	3	=	36
+		−		+		−		
2	+	6	−	3	x	8	=	40
=		=		=		=		
12		16		39		7		

49

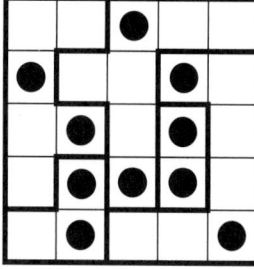

50

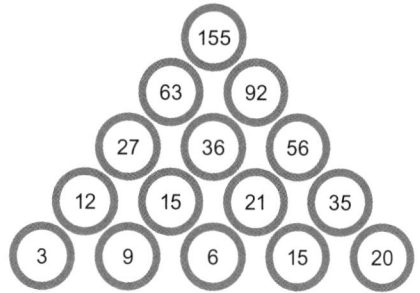

51

9	−	5	x	1	=	4
−		x		+		
3	x	8	+	6	=	30
x		−		x		
7	−	2	x	4	=	20
=		=		=		
42		38		28		

52

476 ÷ 2 = 238,
238 + 32 = 270,
270 ÷ 3 = 90,
40% of 90 = 36,
Square root of 36 = 6,
6 + 15 = 21,
21 ÷ 7 = 3.

53

4	+	8	−	3	x	5	=	45
x		−		+		−		
5	−	4	x	8	+	3	=	11
−		x		x		+		
3	x	5	−	4	+	8	=	19
+		+		−		x		
8	−	3	x	5	+	4	=	29
=		=		=		=		
25		23		39		40		

54

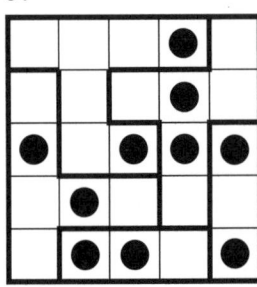

55

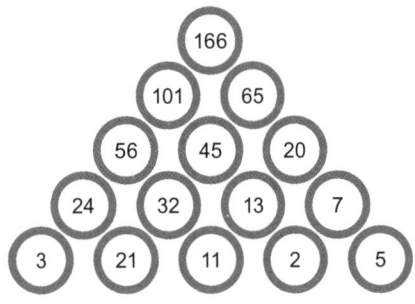

56

4	x	9	−	1	=	35
+		−		x		
7	−	2	x	6	=	30
x		+		−		
5	+	8	−	3	=	10
=		=		=		
55		15		3		

220

57

196 ÷ 4 = 49,
Square root of 49 = 7,
7 + 28 = 35,
35 x 3 = 105,
105 + 29 = 134,
134 ÷ 2 = 67,
67 + 27 = 94.

58

5	+	9	–	8	x	2	=	12
–		+		+		x		
2	x	8	–	5	+	9	=	20
x		x		x		–		
9	–	5	+	2	x	8	=	48
+		–		–		+		
8	–	2	x	9	+	5	=	59
=		=		=		=		
35		83		17		15		

59

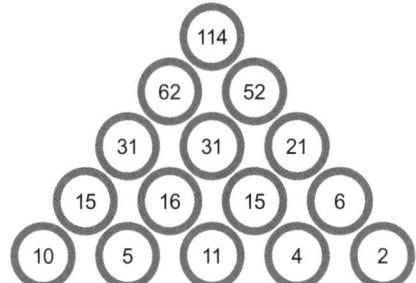

60

61

6	+	8	−	3	=	11
x		+		x		
7	−	2	x	5	=	25
−		x		+		
4	x	9	−	1	=	35
=		=		=		
38		90		16		

62

Cube root of 125 = 5,
5 x 9 = 45,
45 + 13 = 58,
58 ÷ 2 = 29,
29 + 52 = 81,
Square root of 81 = 9,
9 ÷ 3 x 2 = 6.

63

6	−	1	+	7	x	4	=	48
−		x		+		+		
4	x	7	−	1	+	6	=	33
x		−		x		x		
7	−	4	x	6	+	1	=	19
+		+		−		−		
1	+	6	−	4	x	7	=	21
=		=		=		=		
15		9		44		3		

64

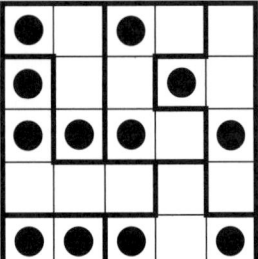

65

```
            183
         101    82
       52    49    33
    25    27    22    11
  16    9    18    4    7
```

66

9	−	1	+	6	=	14
−		+		x		
5	x	3	−	8	=	7
x		x		−		
7	+	2	x	4	=	36
=		=		=		
28		8		44		

67

87 + 9 = 96,
96 ÷ 12 = 8,
8 + 12 = 20,
20 + 1 = 21,
21 ÷ 7 = 3,
3 x 19 = 57,
57 + 73 = 130.

68

5	+	9	x	6	−	8	=	76
+		−		x		+		
6	−	5	x	8	+	9	=	17
−		x		+		−		
9	−	8	+	5	x	6	=	36
x		+		−		x		
8	+	6	−	9	x	5	=	25
=		=		=		=		
16		38		44		55		

69

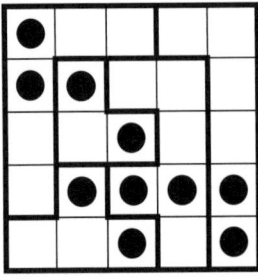

70

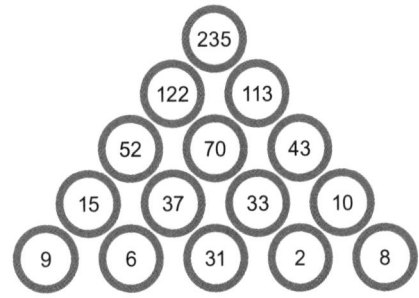

71

5	+	9	−	4	=	10
−		+		x		
2	x	7	+	1	=	15
x		x		+		
3	+	6	x	8	=	72
=		=		=		
9		96		12		

72

$13^2 = 169$,
$169 + 31 = 200$,
$200 ÷ 4 = 50$,
$50 × 5 = 250$,
$250 + 25 = 275$,
$275 − 125 = 150$,
$150 ÷ 3 = 50$.

73

7	−	1	+	3	x	6	=	54
+		+		x		−		
3	+	6	x	7	−	1	=	62
x		x		−		+		
1	x	7	+	6	−	3	=	10
−		−		+		x		
6	−	3	+	1	x	7	=	28
=		=		=		=		
4		46		16		56		

74

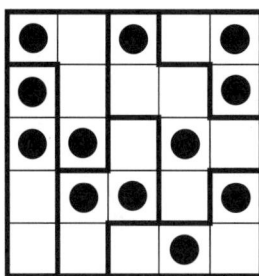

75

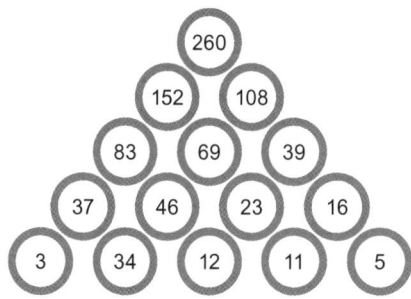

76

4	+	8	x	1	=	12
−		x		+		
2	x	5	−	3	=	7
x		−		x		
9	−	7	+	6	=	8
=		=		=		
18		33		24		

225

77

$75 \times 7 = 525$,
$525 \div 25 = 21$,
$21 \div 7 = 3$,
$3 \times 16 = 48$,
$48 \div 6 = 8$,
$8 \div 4 = 2$,
$2 \times 98 = 196$.

78

7	+	9	–	2	x	3	=	42
–		–		+		x		
2	x	7	–	3	+	9	=	20
x		+		x		–		
9	–	3	x	7	+	2	=	44
+		x		–		+		
3	+	2	x	9	–	7	=	38
=		=		=		=		
48		10		26		32		

79

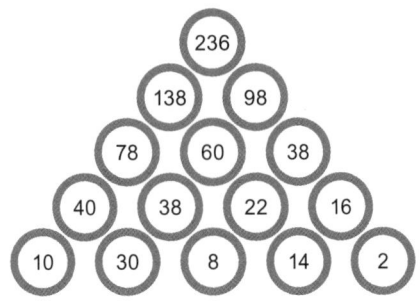

80

81

3	+	2	x	6	=	30
−		x		+		
1	x	8	−	5	=	3
x		+		x		
9	−	4	x	7	=	35
=		=		=		
18		20		77		

82

$76 - 4 = 72$,
$72 \div 8 = 9$,
$9^2 = 81$,
$81 + 39 = 120$,
$120 \div 3 = 40$,
$40 - 4 = 36$,
$36 \div 4 = 9$.

83

5	+	8	−	1	x	6	=	72
−		x		+		x		
1	x	5	+	6	−	8	=	3
x		−		x		−		
8	−	6	x	5	+	1	=	11
+		+		−		+		
6	−	1	+	8	x	5	=	65
=		=		=		=		
38		35		27		52		

84

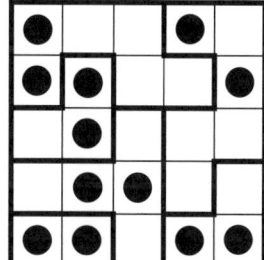

85

- 216
- 108, 108
- 56, 52, 56
- 27, 29, 23, 33
- 12, 15, 14, 9, 24

86

5	−	1	x	3	=	12
+		x		+		
8	x	6	−	7	=	41
x		−		x		
4	−	2	x	9	=	18
=		=		=		
52		4		90		

87

$48 \div 4 = 12$,
$12 + 114 = 126$,
$126 \div 6 = 21$,
$21 - 15 = 6$,
$6 + 7 = 13$,
$13^2 = 169$,
$169 + 31 = 200$.

88

4	x	6	−	8	+	5	=	21
+		−		−		x		
8	−	5	x	4	+	6	=	18
−		x		x		−		
6	+	8	−	5	x	4	=	36
x		+		+		+		
5	−	4	x	6	+	8	=	14
=		=		=		=		
30		12		26		34		

89

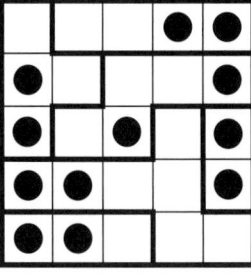

90

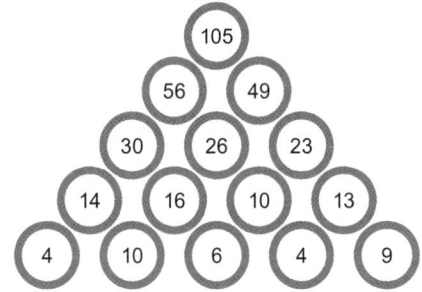

91

4	+	2	x	5	=	30
+		x		−		
6	+	9	−	3	=	12
−		+		x		
8	−	1	x	7	=	49
=		=		=		
2		19		14		

92

$47 - 38 = 9$,
$9^2 = 81$,
$81 \div 3 = 27$,
$27 + 9 = 36$,
Square root of $36 = 6$,
$6 \times 7 = 42$,
$42 - 18 = 24$.

93

3	x	7	−	5	+	2	=	18
+		−		x		+		
5	−	2	x	7	+	3	=	24
x		x		−		x		
2	+	5	x	3	−	7	=	14
−		+		+		−		
7	+	3	x	2	−	5	=	15
=		=		=		=		
9		28		34		30		

94

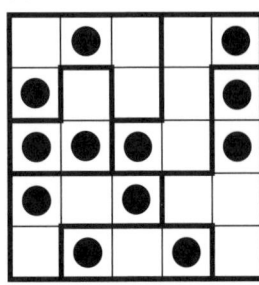

95

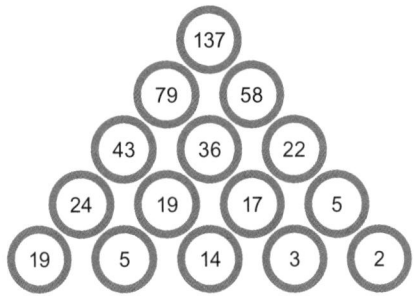

96

9	−	2	+	7	=	14
−		+		−		
4	+	8	−	3	=	9
x		x		+		
1	x	6	+	5	=	11
=		=		=		
5		60		9		

230

97

$10 \div 5 \times 2 = 4$,
$4^2 = 16$,
$16 \div 4 \times 3 = 12$,
$12 \times 9 = 108$,
$108 \div 6 = 18$,
$18 + 48 = 66$,
$66 \div 3 = 22$.

98

3	+	8	x	2	−	7	=	15
−		−		+		+		
2	+	7	−	3	x	8	=	48
+		+		x		x		
7	−	3	+	8	x	2	=	24
x		x		−		−		
8	x	2	−	7	+	3	=	12
=		=		=		=		
64		8		33		27		

99

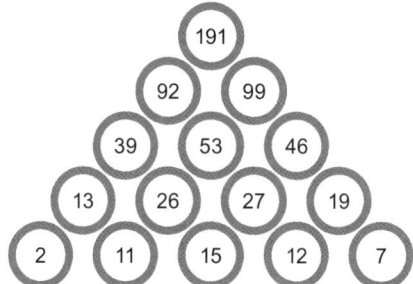

100

101

4	x	9	−	6	=	30
x		+		−		
3	+	7	x	1	=	10
+		−		+		
8	−	5	x	2	=	6
=		=		=		
20		11		7		

102

$94 - 16 = 78$,
$78 \div 2 = 39$,
$39 \div 3 \times 2 = 26$,
$26 + 14 = 40$,
$40 \div 5 \times 3 = 24$,
$24 \times 3 = 72$,
$72 + 28 = 100$.

103

3	+	7	−	9	x	6	=	6
x		−		+		x		
9	−	3	x	6	+	7	=	43
+		x		−		−		
6	x	9	+	7	−	3	=	58
−		+		x		+		
7	−	6	+	3	x	9	=	36
=		=		=		=		
26		42		24		48		

104

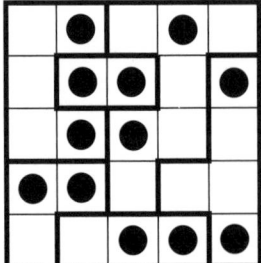

105

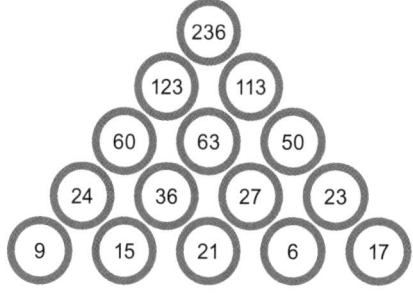

106

3	+	7	x	1	=	10
x		−		+		
6	−	5	x	9	=	9
+		x		x		
8	x	4	+	2	=	34
=		=		=		
26		8		20		

107

60% of 200 = 120,
120 ÷ 4 = 30,
30 + 10 = 40,
40 x 4 = 160,
160 ÷ 20 = 8,
8 x 11 = 88,
88 − 42 = 46.

108

5	+	9	x	3	−	6	=	36
−		x		x		+		
3	x	5	−	6	+	9	=	18
x		−		+		x		
9	+	6	x	5	−	3	=	72
+		+		−		−		
6	−	3	x	9	+	5	=	32
=		=		=		=		
24		42		14		40		

109

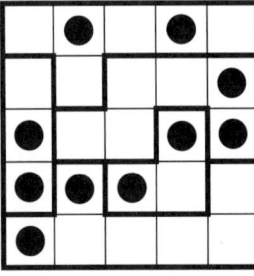

110

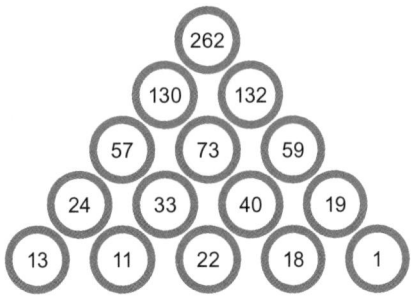

111

3	x	6	−	9	=	9
+		−		+		
2	+	5	x	7	=	49
x		x		x		
8	−	1	+	4	=	11
=		=		=		
40		1		64		

112

$2^2 = 4$,
$4 \times 9 = 36$,
Square root of $36 = 6$,
$6 \times 7 = 42$,
$42 \div 3 = 14$,
$14 + 8 = 22$,
$22 + 38 = 60$.

113

5	+	7	−	2	x	9	=	90
−		+		x		−		
2	x	5	+	9	−	7	=	12
x		x		−		+		
9	−	2	x	7	+	5	=	54
+		−		+		x		
7	+	9	x	5	−	2	=	78
=		=		=		=		
34		15		16		14		

114

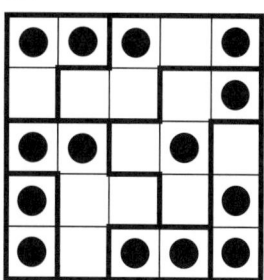

115

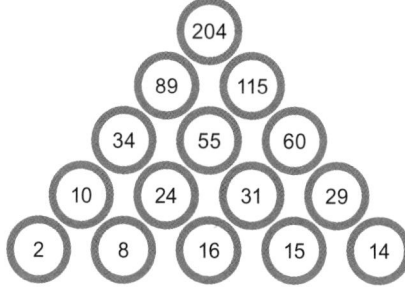

116

2	+	7	−	5	=	4
+		−		x		
6	x	3	−	8	=	10
x		+		−		
9	−	1	x	4	=	32
=		=		=		
72		5		36		

117

$31 - 15 = 16$,
$16 + 4 = 20$,
$20 + 18 = 38$,
$38 \div 2 = 19$,
$19 - 11 = 8$,
$8^2 = 64$,
$64 + 146 = 210$.

118

5	+	9	x	2	–	7	=	21
–		–		+		+		
2	x	5	–	7	+	9	=	12
+		x		x		x		
7	–	2	x	9	+	5	=	50
x		+		–		–		
9	+	7	–	5	x	2	=	22
=		=		=		=		
90		15		76		78		

119

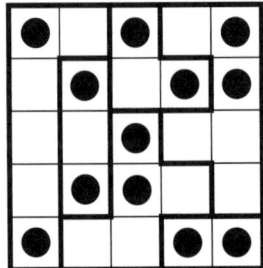

120

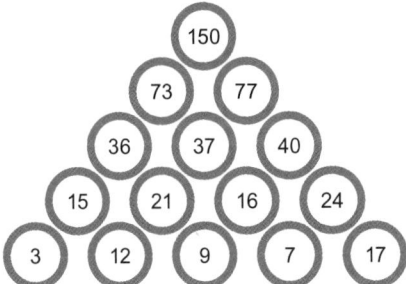

121

9	−	3	x	8	=	48
+		x		−		
2	+	6	x	5	=	40
x		−		x		
7	+	4	−	1	=	10
=		=		=		
77		14		3		

122

$35 \div 5 = 7$,
$7 + 27 = 34$,
$34 \times 2 = 68$,
$68 \div 4 = 17$,
$17 - 8 = 9$,
Square root of $9 = 3$,
$3 \times 15 = 45$.

123

9	−	3	+	1	x	8	=	56
+		x		+		−		
1	x	9	−	8	+	3	=	4
x		−		x		+		
3	+	8	x	9	−	1	=	98
−		+		−		x		
8	−	1	+	3	x	9	=	90
=		=		=		=		
22		20		78		54		

124

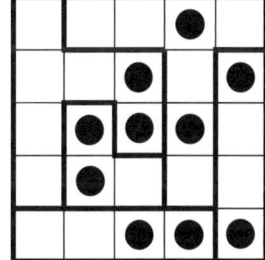

125

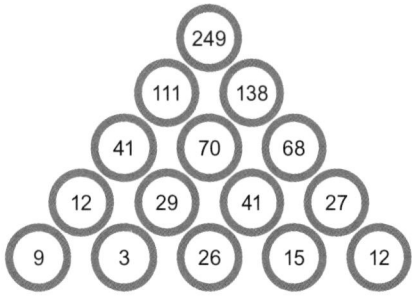

126

4	+	1	x	7	=	35
x		+		−		
6	+	8	−	2	=	12
−		x		+		
3	x	5	+	9	=	24
=		=		=		
21		45		14		

127

90 ÷ 5 = 18,
18 ÷ 3 x 2 = 12,
12 ÷ 4 x 3 = 9,
9 x 8 = 72,
72 + 28 = 100,
100 + 20 = 120,
120 ÷ 3 = 40.

128

2	+	8	x	5	−	4	=	46
x		−		−		+		
5	x	4	−	2	+	8	=	26
−		+		x		x		
4	+	2	x	8	−	5	=	43
+		x		+		−		
8	x	5	+	4	−	2	=	42
=		=		=		=		
14		30		28		58		

129

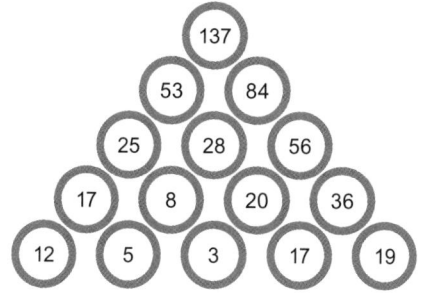

130

Pyramid:
- 137
- 53, 84
- 25, 28, 56
- 17, 8, 20, 36
- 12, 5, 3, 17, 19

131

8	x	3	+	6	=	30
−		+		x		
5	+	2	x	7	=	49
+		x		−		
1	+	9	x	4	=	40
=		=		=		
4		45		38		

132

56 + 15 = 71,
71 − 7 = 64,
64 ÷ 4 = 16,
Square root of 16 = 4,
4 + 69 = 73,
73 − 14 = 59,
59 + 23 = 82.

133

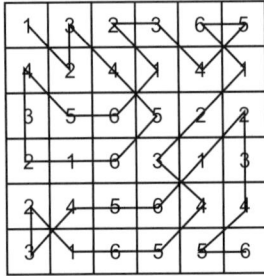

134

The values of the letters in the outer squares are added to give the value of the letter in the central square. Thus the missing value is 16, so the missing letter is P.

135

12 – Each higher number is 12 times the number on the opposite point of the star.

136

9	−	1	+	4	=	12
−		+		x		
3	+	7	x	5	=	50
+		x		−		
2	x	6	+	8	=	20
=		=		=		
8		48		12		

137

4	4	4	2	2	4
3	2	2	1	1	3
3	2	2	1	1	3
2	3	3	2	2	1
2	3	3	2	2	1
2	3	3	4	4	3

138

55 ÷ 11 x 4 = 20,
20 x 1.75 = 35,
35 ÷ 7 x 2 = 10,
400% of 10 = 40,
40 + 47 = 87,
87 ÷ 3 x 2 = 58,
58 ÷ 0.5 = 116.

139

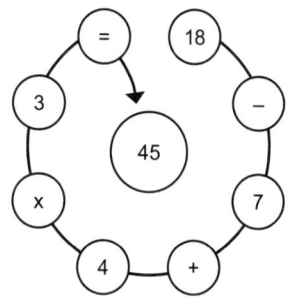

140

B – Working from top left to top right, then to bottom left, then to bottom right, each group of nine squares makes a quarter turn clockwise.

141

Clocks gain 42½ minutes each time.

142

							119
22	30	1	18	23	6	21	121
24	12	20	27	16	24	15	138
7	17	22	11	3	20	30	110
23	4	29	17	28	9	22	132
25	1	16	2	29	28	26	127
8	26	14	18	25	10	27	128
12	13	19	11	5	19	21	100
121	103	121	104	129	116	162	133

143

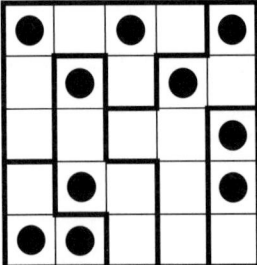

144

Circle = 6,
Cross = 2,
Pentagon = 3,
Square = 8,
Star = 7.

145

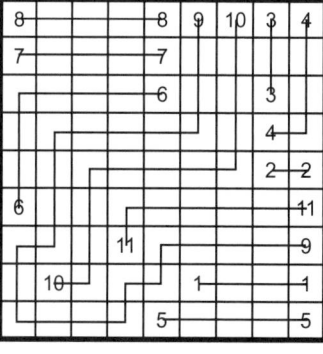

146

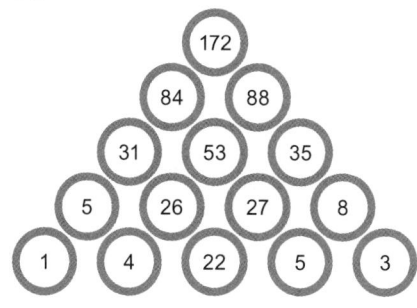

147

4	+	3	x	9	−	6	=	57
x		+		−		+		
6	−	4	+	3	x	9	=	45
−		x		+		x		
9	−	6	x	4	+	3	=	15
+		−		x		−		
3	x	9	−	6	+	4	=	25
=		=		=		=		
18		33		60		41		

148

4	5	8	4	■	4	5	1	1
0	■		3	7	8	0	■	0
7	8	9	1	■	8	9	0	4
7	8	4	1	9	0	3	■	0
■	5	5	■	6	■	2	2	■
1	■	6	2	2	3	8	7	3
5	2	2	3	■	1	0	8	4
4	■	2	8	4	7	■		3
4	5	5	6	■	4	8	9	2

149

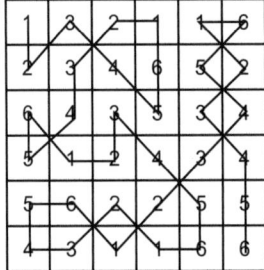

150

The value of the letter in the top right square is subtracted from the sum total of the values of the letters in the top left, bottom left and bottom right squares to give the value of the letter in the central square. Thus the missing value is 24, so the missing letter is X.

151

5 – Each higher number is double the number on the opposite point of the star, plus five.

152

4	x	3	–	7	=	5
+		x		+		
1	x	6	+	9	=	15
x		+		–		
8	–	5	x	2	=	6
=		=		=		
40		23		14		

153

4	2	2	1	1	2
2	1	1	3	3	2
2	1	1	3	3	2
2	4	4	4	4	3
2	4	4	4	4	3
4	1	1	2	2	3

154

2222 ÷ 11 = 202,
150% of 202 = 303,
303 + 30 = 333,
333 ÷ 37 x 5 = 45,
45 ÷ 15 = 3,
3 ÷ 3 x 2 = 2,
2 x 86 = 172.

155

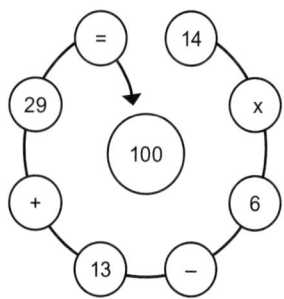

156

D – Working from left to right across each row of three squares, add two each time to the numbers in the top row, three to the numbers in the middle row, and four to the numbers in the bottom row.

157

Clocks lose 40 minutes, 50 minutes, 60 minutes and 70 minutes each time.

158

							103
15	16	7	20	6	15	18	97
25	2	27	30	22	29	29	164
2	12	23	4	26	3	26	96
4	8	24	13	25	23	14	111
21	21	2	30	1	17	11	103
22	5	28	28	19	3	10	115
10	12	24	9	19	29	24	127
99	76	135	134	118	119	132	81

159

160

Circle = 1,
Cross = 2,
Pentagon = 7,
Square = 5,
Star = 9.

161

162

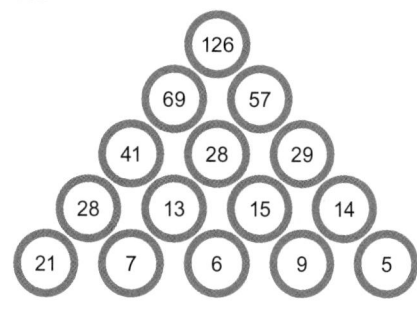

163

9	−		+	4	×	7	=	70
×		+		+		−		
4	+	7	×	9	−	3	=	96
−		×		−		×		
7	×	9	−	3	+	4	=	64
+		−		×		+		
3	+	4	×	7	−	9	=	40
=		=		=		=		
32		86		70		25		

164

5	8	9	3	■	6	7	4	5
3	■	4	3	1	2	8	■	0
1	6	5	0	■	2	6	7	2
8	0	0	■	6	7	2	8	0
■	3	■	1	0	1	■	4	■
3	6	9	4	0	■	8	7	2
7	5	8	3	■	4	1	5	9
7	■	3	0	3	9	2	■	4
8	7	1	9	■	4	6	6	8

165

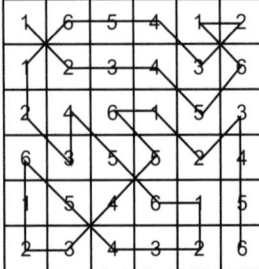

166

The value of the letter in the top right square is subtracted from the value of the letter in the top left square, to give the value of the letter in the bottom left square. The value of the letter in the bottom right square is then subtracted from the value of the letter in the bottom left square, to give the value of the letter in the central square. Thus the missing value is 1, so the missing letter is A.

167

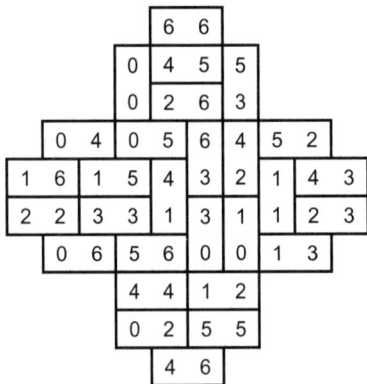

168

4	5	1	2	3
2	4	3	1	5
1	3	4	5	2
5	1	2	3	4
3	2	5	4	1

248

169

4	+	7	x	2	=	22
−		+		x		
1	x	6	+	8	=	14
x		−		+		
5	+	9	−	3	=	11
=		=		=		
15		4		19		

170
7443

171

1S	1S	2S	1E	2W
2S	1E	1E	1N	1S
2N	2N	■	1S	1W
1E	1N	1S	1W	2N
2N	2E	2W	1E	1N

172

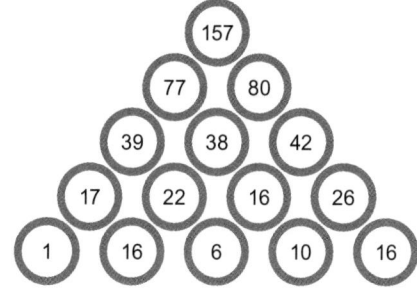

173

D	E	F	C	B	A
C	B	E	A	F	D
B	F	C	D	A	E
E	A	D	F	C	B
A	C	B	E	D	F
F	D	A	B	E	C

174

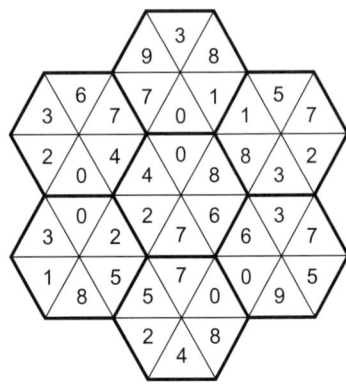

175

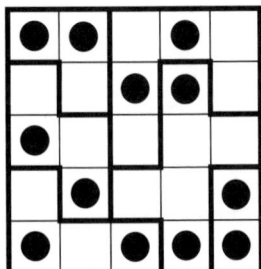

176

177

34	9	12	19	40	22
27	22	28	11	26	22
24	32	22	28	7	23
21	38	26	16	15	20
18	22	17	36	18	25
12	13	31	26	30	24

178

$247 \div 13 \times 3 = 57$,
$57 \div 19 \times 5 = 15$,
$15 \times 35 = 525$,
$525 \div 21 \times 5 = 125$,
Cube root of $125 = 5$,
$5 \times 1.4 = 7$,
$7 \times 45 = 315$.

179

9	−	4	x	7	+	6	=	41
+		x		−		x		
6	+	9	x	4	−	7	=	53
−		−		+		−		
4	x	7	−	6	+	9	=	31
x		+		x		+		
7	−	6	+	9	x	4	=	40
=		=		=		=		
77		35		81		35		

180

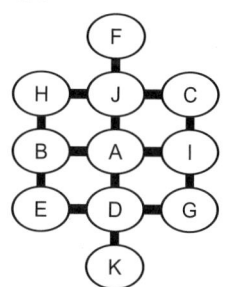

181

Other solutions may be possible.

182

9	3	7	2	5	1	8	4	6
1	6	4	3	9	8	5	2	7
5	8	2	4	6	7	3	1	9
2	9	8	7	3	5	1	6	4
3	4	5	1	2	6	9	7	8
7	1	6	9	8	4	2	5	3
8	7	9	6	1	2	4	3	5
4	2	3	5	7	9	6	8	1
6	5	1	8	4	3	7	9	2

183

184

5	4	3	1	2
2	3	5	4	1
1	2	4	3	5
4	5	1	2	3
3	1	2	5	4

252

185

9	−	2	x	5	=	35
x		+		−		
4	+	7	x	1	=	11
−		x		x		
3	x	8	−	6	=	18
=		=		=		
33		72		24		

186
7534

187

1S	2E	2W	1E	2S
1E	2S	1N	2S	1W
1S	2N	■	2S	2W
2E	1N	2N	1N	2N
2N	1E	2W	2W	1N

188

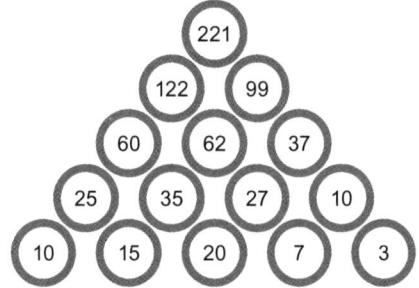

189

D	A	B	F	E	C
E	C	A	D	F	B
C	D	F	E	B	A
B	E	D	A	C	F
A	F	C	B	D	E
F	B	E	C	A	D

190

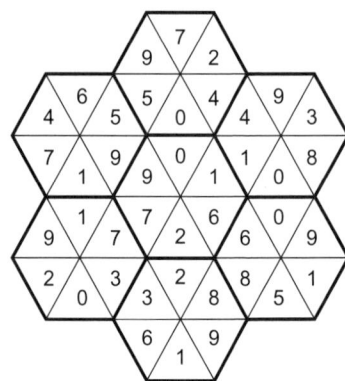

191

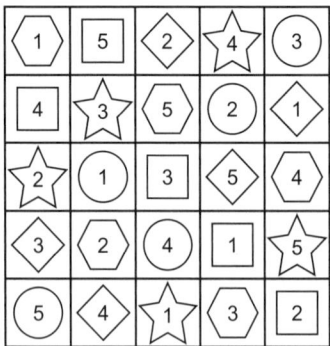

192

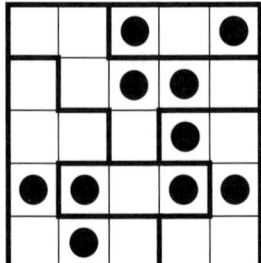

193

16	11	13	18	27	16
22	16	18	9	21	15
15	28	16	20	9	13
18	27	21	12	5	18
13	6	19	23	21	19
17	13	14	19	18	20

194
33 x 25 = 825,
825 ÷ 3 x 2 = 550,
550 ÷ 11 x 9 = 450,
28% of 450 = 126,
126 ÷ 14 x 5 = 45,
45 + 89 = 134,
134 ÷ 0.25 = 536.

195

3	+	8	−	7	x	5	=	20
x		−		x		+		
5	x	7	+	8	−	3	=	40
+		x		−		x		
7	+	3	x	5	−	8	=	42
−		+		+		−		
8	−	5	x	3	+	7	=	16
=		=		=		=		
14		8		54		57		

196

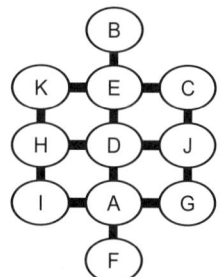

197

Other solutions may be possible.

198

8	3	1	6	4	9	2	7	5
5	9	6	8	7	2	4	1	3
4	7	2	3	1	5	6	8	9
2	8	7	4	9	1	3	5	6
6	1	3	5	2	8	9	4	7
9	4	5	7	3	6	1	2	8
3	5	9	1	8	4	7	6	2
1	2	8	9	6	7	5	3	4
7	6	4	2	5	3	8	9	1

199

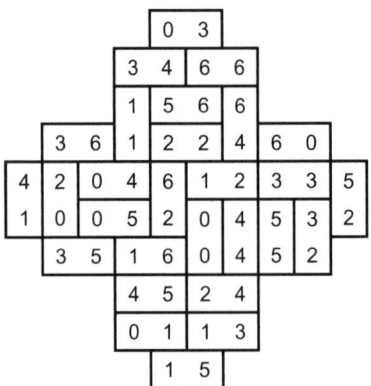

200

4	5	3	1	2
3	2	4	5	1
1	4	2	3	5
5	3	1	2	4
2	1	5	4	3